Praise

'These are without doubt the best self-help practices you'll ever do. Practical, simple and life changing. It makes a huge difference when you implement the advice, and you get to understand yourself and others at a deep level. It is life changing.'
— **Lois Baxter Smallwood**, Hospitality Management, Peak District, UK

'*The Seven-Day Positivity Project* is amazing and full of golden nuggets to help you move away from negativity and focus on the positives. It takes very little time, approximately 15 minutes a day, and without a doubt, it can truly help change your mindset. My favourite tool is the black dot. It's amazing how something so simple can make such a difference, particularly if life is feeling difficult. Thank you for sharing such a wonderful gift.'
— **Bridget Keady Munro**, Community Funding and Engagement Officer, Cambridge, UK

'This is a wonderful project in supporting self-care. It provides you with tools to self-regulate and allows joy into your life. Thank you, Moira.'
— **Fiona Higgins**, Reflexologist and QTT® Practitioner, Waterville, Co Kerry, Ireland

'*The Seven-Day Positivity Project* is the best project I have ever done. Life changing and all for the better.'
— **Ailish Malone**, Artist, Kilrush, Co Clare, Ireland

The Seven-Day Positivity Project

A surprisingly easy way to feel better no matter what!

MOIRA GEARY

R^ethink

First published in Great Britain in 2024
by Rethink Press (www.rethinkpress.com)

© Copyright Moira Geary

All rights reserved. No part of this publication may be reproduced, stored in or introduced into a retrieval system, or transmitted, in any form, or by any means (electronic, mechanical, photocopying, recording or otherwise) without the prior written permission of the publisher.

The right of Moira Geary to be identified as the author of this work has been asserted by her in accordance with the Copyright, Designs and Patents Act 1988.

This book is sold subject to the condition that it shall not, by way of trade or otherwise, be lent, resold, hired out, or otherwise circulated without the publisher's prior consent in any form of binding or cover other than that in which it is published and without a similar condition including this condition being imposed on the subsequent purchaser.

Disclaimer

Please note that the information contained in this book is not intended as a substitute for professional medical advice, diagnosis or treatment. Reliance on any information or guidance provided in the content is solely at your own risk. The publisher will not be held liable in any way for any effects that result from the use of the content.

This book is dedicated to every person on the planet seeking to live the good life that they deserve.

Contents

Introduction   1
    A seven-day journey   2

Prologue: My Story   7
    What happened next   13

1 Before You Start...   15
    It doesn't have to be hard   16
    Positive psychology   23
    Summary   24

2 Day One: The Power Of Your Mind   27
    Your conscious mind   28
    Your subconscious mind   31
    Chin up – why physiology matters   36
    Gratitude   40

	Positive expectations	43
	Summary	45
3	**Day Two: Take Control**	**47**
	Association/disassociation	47
	Mind–body connection	50
	Managing problems	52
	Golden Rule 1: Change your perception of reality	55
	Summary	58
4	**Day Three: Order Out Of Chaos**	**59**
	Fear	59
	The process of worry	62
	Overwhelm	65
	Procrastination	69
	Golden Rule 2: Everyone has their own unique model of the world	72
	Summary	74
5	**Day Four: Why We Do What We Do**	**75**
	The Seven Behavioural Codes	76
	Code 1: Sureness	79
	Code 2: Diversity	80
	Code 3: Importance	82
	Code 4: Love	86

Code 5: Authentic voice 88
Code 6: Evolution 89
Code 7: Connection 90
Golden Rule 3: There is a positive intention behind all behaviour 92
Summary 93

6 Day Five: Influences Of Our Past 95
Memories and beliefs 95
Values: What is important? 102
What is the meaning of it all? 105
Golden Rule 4: Practise non-judgement of others 107
Summary 110

7 Day Six: Making The Most Of Mini Miens 113
Introducing the Mini Miens 113
Identifying the Mini Miens 115
Listening to the Mini Miens 124
Golden Rule 5: You have all the resources you need 126
Summary 127

8 Day Seven: Making A Habit Of It 129
Physical and emotional habits 130
Feelings call the shots 132

Golden Rule 6: People can only meet you where they are	138
Summary	142

9 Onwards And Upwards   **145**

Embracing change	145
Your 'why'	146
Your vision	149
Getting your ducks in a row	151
Get to the detail	153
Action in action	158
Summary	160

Conclusion   **163**

Work with me	164
My final message	164

Notes   **167**

Acknowledgements   **173**

The Author   **175**

Introduction

Welcome to *The Seven-Day Positivity Project*, a transformative guide designed to unlock positivity and empower you on a journey towards a more positive and fulfilling life. In a world that often feels overwhelming, challenging and filled with uncertainties, this book is your companion to navigate the intricacies of your mind and emotions, providing you with practical tools to cultivate lasting positivity.

We all experience a myriad of challenges, both internal and external. Whether it's dealing with negative thought patterns, facing emotional struggles, managing difficult relationships or feeling stuck in your comfort zone, *The Seven-Day Positivity Project* addresses these hurdles head-on. This book recognises the complexities of daily life and offers a structured, actionable approach to help you overcome your challenges.

The Seven-Day Positivity Project is not just a book; it's a dynamic programme designed to create real, tangible change in your life. By committing to and embarking on this seven-day journey, you will be equipped with a powerful set of tools, both practical skills and transformative insights, including:

- Enhanced emotional intelligence
- Effective relationship strategies
- Expanded comfort zone
- Positive language mastery
- Compassionate connection

A seven-day journey

Each day of the programme corresponds to a chapter in the book, offering a seamless integration of insights, exercises and practices. This carefully orchestrated progression builds upon previous days, facilitating the organic development of positive habits, and empowering you to confront life's challenges with unwavering resilience and optimism.

INTRODUCTION

Day One: The Power Of Your Mind

- Harness the power of the conscious and subconscious mind to help support your best life.

- Introduction to the reticular activating system (RAS): unleash the power of focus by understanding and harnessing the RAS.

- Cultivate awareness and the positive impact of physiology.

- Discover the use of expectations and their profound impact on shaping your reality.

Day Two: Take Control

- The role of association and disassociation in shaping reality: delve into understanding the influence these two elements have on your mindset.

- Uncover the nuances of the mind–body connection and how to adapt these elements to self-regulate.

- Learn the Problem Not Problem® technique to support you in the management of any problem.

Day Three: Order Out Of Chaos

- Unravel the process of worry and apply exercises to empower you to navigate life's fears and challenges.

- Uncover the signs of overwhelm and transform them into logical order.

- Recognise the triggers of procrastination and what to do to change them.

Day Four: Why We Do What We Do

- Understand the Seven Behavioural Codes®: decode the patterns governing your behaviour and learn to wield them consciously.

- Cultivate compassion and understanding in relationships by embracing diverse perspectives on why people behave the way they do.

- Maintain personal power in challenging interactions.

- Protect emotional wellbeing in difficult relationships.

Day Five: Influences Of Our Past

- Understand the role of beliefs and memories and learn how to use them for best results.

- Use the power of what you value most in life to shape your best future.
- Recognise how the meaning we put on our reality has the power to change our reality so choose wisely.

Day Six: Making The Most Of Mini Miens

- Introduction to the power of your Mini Miens and how to use them to change your state.
- Instigate change by learning to access the resources within you that can support your desired change.

Day Seven: Making A Habit Of It

- Discover how habits get formed and why they are important pillars of a happy life.
- Recognise the profound impact emotions have on our behaviour and how to harness them for best results.
- Recognise the confines of your comfort zone and embark on a journey of expansion.
- Learn the Pink Bow technique for emotional regulation and resilience.

The Seven-Day Positivity Project is not just a guide; it's a holistic program designed to empower you to create lasting positive change. As you embark on this journey, remember that transformation is a process, and each day brings new opportunities to build a life filled with purpose, joy and resilience. Get ready to unlock the doors to positivity and step into a brighter, more fulfilling future. The journey starts now.

Prologue: My Story

I get it.

I know that we all have experienced worry, fear, stress, overwhelm, self-doubt and low self-confidence at times. However, I also know these feelings don't have to affect us to the extent that they often do, and I am passionate about supporting as many people as I possibly can to avoid the pain that these feelings cause. You may wonder why you should listen to me. You don't have to, but thousands of people who have, have attained the positive results they were looking for. My techniques and processes worked for them, and they can work for you, too.

As a former nurse and midwife with a master's degree in psychotherapy and a higher diploma in positive health, I have done the groundwork to understand the science behind my approach. It's not just academic and scientific qualifications that qualify me to speak to you about positivity but also, and more importantly, over twenty-five years of experience working with clients in the personal development space, and the results they have achieved.

Throughout the years, I have witnessed thousands of people like you transform the way they were feeling and thinking, which helped them to flourish and thrive regardless of their situation. Yes, some people's situations can be particularly difficult, but I have watched them learn how to release their fear, worry and overwhelm, and grow in confidence and self-esteem so that they can live their best lives.

That said, there is another, even more important reason why you might listen to me: I have experienced some extremely difficult periods in my life and have overcome them with the help of many of the ideas and techniques that you will find in this book.

The first and most debilitating of these experiences was when I was in a state of anxiety that tipped me into a depressed state. I was put on medication to help relieve my symptoms, but it exacerbated my symptoms and I had to come off it (in retrospect, I am thankful for this).

PROLOGUE: MY STORY

After attending multiple sessions with three different counsellors and seeing no improvement, I felt I had no option but to work through the depressed state in my own way and bring myself to a place where I could experience happiness, joy and peace again. I know I will never go back to the bleakness that I endured every moment of every day for four solid years. It was this experience of anxiety, overwhelm and fear – and being in a deep state of hopelessness – that helps me to understand my clients and create my Quantum Thinking Transformation® (QTT®) methodology, much of which I share in this book.

I find it difficult to express the depth of the pain I endured when I was feeling that low. Often, when you are feeling anxious, sad, hopeless, lonely, fearful or overwhelmed, people can't see it on the outside, although you feel it deeply on the inside. At the time, I had no idea why I was so desperate, which made me feel disempowered and helpless. I understand now that my anxious state stemmed from the deep beliefs I had about my ability to achieve. I had failed three important exams in my late teens and early twenties. This dented my confidence hugely and resulted in me subconsciously creating deep-rooted negative beliefs and feelings of shame around not being good enough, smart enough, disciplined enough... the list goes on.

Before I failed these exams, I had enjoyed much acknowledgement and praise, especially from my dad. I got this validation when I worked hard and achieved results both academically and in practical projects. That feeling of being acknowledged or praised was tremendous. I respected my dad so much that when I got his approval for doing something well, I wanted to experience that feeling again and again. Striving for his approval so that I could feel good became an automatic subconscious behavioural pattern, and it was working well for me.

But then when I failed academically, the feelings of personal shame and disappointment became deeply ingrained. I started to believe that I was not good enough and began to create many other negative and disempowering beliefs about myself. While of course a simplistic explanation, there were a few key factors that particularly influenced this disempowering pattern, the depth of the effect of which I did not appreciate until many years later.

When I was in my mid-to-late thirties I decided to create my own skin care business. I developed products and devised the brand and the marketing strategy myself with ease. I was delighted with the products and I was immensely proud of what I had created. It was not until I had to go out and sell them that I started to experience feelings of discomfort. This was the first time since my late teenage years that I'd had to sell 'me' – I was asking people to invest in me and something I had created. Before long, the fear of rejection began to creep in.

It started slowly, but I would notice on waking in the morning that I was feeling a touch of anxiety in my solar plexus (high up in my tummy and just below my breastbone). Over time, the feeling intensified and became more prolonged and debilitating. This continued until I felt the fear and anxiety at a high level all day. Despite these crippling feelings, I was determined not to give up, as I believed that this would be even more shameful than the fear of selling myself.

Any time I had to push myself to sell or promote my products, I would feel the intensity of the anxiety rise. I remember one particular afternoon when I sat in front of my computer and just stared at it for three hours. I was paralysed by fear and my inability to manage the anxiety. It was so bad I had to call my husband, Jeff, and ask him to come home.

What happened next is what happens to many people dealing with anxiety. In my despair at not being able to manage my feelings, I quickly sank into a hopeless and depressed state. I found it difficult to get out of bed in the morning. Even the most basic of self-care tasks, like taking a shower or cooking a meal, were a struggle. To be in this state and feel that there was no way out, no relief and no way of reducing the intensity of the pain, was terrifying and utterly crippling. I had no choice but to take myself in hand and slowly find my way through.

As a family, we have experienced other difficult situations, including the wiping out of our household income overnight as a result of the recession, which came just weeks after my mother-in-law went missing on a holiday in Italy.

This was a devastating time for us. To my mind, this type of thing only happened to people on TV, not ordinary people like us. Not knowing what had happened to granny and not being able to take part in the search was extremely frustrating and upsetting. We had to wait for eighteen months for closure with the discovery of her remains so that we could have a funeral and grieve.

While all of that was going on, the construction industry in Ireland was on its knees. It was looking bleak, employment-wise, for Jeff. To find our way through, we had to put every aspect and technique of *The Seven-Day Positivity Project* into action.

The reason I was able to manage is that I had already taught myself many of the techniques and practices I will be sharing with you in this book. I had, in effect, created tools to support myself and others around me. These were instrumental in helping to bring me out of my anxious state, and in how we, as a family, managed our grief and our financial problems.

In many ways, the challenging situations were a positive force, helping us to evolve and grow, but I know it would have been much more difficult without these techniques and learnings.

What happened next

I've always had a keen interest in what makes people tick. There were people in my circle who needed help; I worked with them, sharing elements of what I had done to free myself, and they started to get their own great results. It was a fantastic feeling.

I then started working one to one with clients, but soon saw that this was limiting my capacity to help more people. I realised that holding live events would increase the reach of my message, and that expanded quickly to include supporting people online. To date, I have been able to support over 20,000 people in following the Seven-Day Positivity Project methodology so that they can live calmer and more enriched lives. Our supportive community continues to grow daily, and you are welcome to join it (for free) – simply visit www.moirageary.com/community and request to join.

Whether it is your relationships, career, finances, health, business or spiritual growth that are suffering, if you follow my step-by-step methodology and implement the lessons, you are guaranteed to feel better. Doing this is a gift to yourself and others. When you have the power to regulate your emotions in an instant and keep yourself calm and in control in any situation, you have a profoundly positive impact on the people around you.

Thankfully, in recent times, we have begun to experience a shift towards people taking responsibility for their own happiness. It is a movement that is exciting to be part of – and you don't need to wait for someone to invite you along; you can row in yourself and join the action.

In all my years of practice, I have never met a committed client who reverted to their old disempowering ways. Positive change helps people to live better lives, but sustainable change is even more powerful and helps people to live *exceptional* lives.

Your power lives within you. You will not be able to access this power from anything outside of you. It's not that things outside of you won't affect you, but your happiness cannot be found outside of you. This is an inside job. Once we know it is possible to be happier, we have a responsibility to do and be our best. This book will show you how.

The Seven-Day Positivity Project is not just a guide; it's a holistic programme designed to empower you to create lasting positive change. As you embark on this journey, remember that transformation is a process, and each day brings new opportunities to build a life filled with purpose, joy and resilience. Get ready to unlock the doors to positivity and step into a brighter, more fulfilling future. The journey starts now.

ONE
Before You Start...

Before I introduce the concepts of the Seven-Day Positivity Project, it's important to set you up to get the best results. If you are feeling in any way under siege from a barrage of disconnected thoughts, indecision, comparison, self-criticism, fear, worries and stresses, but you hope to become happier and more successful, this chapter is critical. It will make sure that you are sufficiently prepared to get off to a strong start and that you have everything you need for success.

Sadly, most of us don't know what we need to get us even half-way towards achieving confidence, calmness, clarity, focus, peace and joy. We are so busy feeling overwhelmed and fearful that we are not even aware that we are stuck in the same old patterns, day in and day out. We are conditioned to accept our lot and we think that this is 'just the way life is'. It isn't.

It doesn't have to be hard

I want you to learn how to feel your best in any situation, no matter what is happening around you. I want you to feel alive and purposeful. I want you to feel empowered to live the good life you truly deserve. I want you to embrace the idea that life does not always have to be as difficult as we make it. I want you to learn all of this because when you do, your world will change for the better, for you and everyone else in your life – your family, friends, intimate partners, children, acquaintances and even your pets.

Many years ago, when I started my personal development journey, the consensus was that creating effective and lasting behavioural and emotional change was difficult and would most likely take a long time. This is not true. Profound and lasting change can be quick, and it can be easy – if you learn how to do it in the right way. After all, some of our biggest fears have been learned in a moment: perhaps you were made to feel uncomfortable in school when you had to read aloud in front of your class, or maybe you were confronted by an angry dog and had a panic reaction. Both these situations can set up intense fear responses that can stay with you for life, yet they were acquired instantly. Our nervous system is just as capable of unlearning those same fear responses.[1] Witnessing this happen is a joyful experience. As you implement the simple techniques that I'll be showing you over the next seven days, you'll see just how quick and easy emotional change can be.

All I ask is that you actually implement these techniques. I'm not going to ask you to do anything difficult, nor does it need to be twenty-four hours a day. I'm just asking for enough implementation to allow you to experience positive change. At the risk of repeating myself, implementation is not hard; in fact, it can be fun and easy.

The importance of habits

We are not born with habits; we develop them over time. A habit is just a way of behaving that becomes our usual way. Habits are responsible for how we feel and how we behave, as well as our results in life.

Before we look more closely at habits and their potential to help us live our best lives, we need to understand that they are neither good nor bad, neither right nor wrong. They are just habits. The way we become discerning about which ones we want to develop and which we wish to change is by asking ourselves, 'Does this habit serve me?' If you have habits of worry, stress, being overwhelmed or procrastinating, you probably feel that they don't serve or support you in how you want to live your life – and you would be right. This is a good place to start our change.

As you move through this book and implement the techniques, you will be unlearning old habits and embedding new ones, which will change your reactive behaviours as well as your stress responses in difficult situations.

The process of embedding new habits, patterns of behaviour and skills comprises four distinct steps, according to Noel Burch's Stages of Competence model:[2]

- **Step One:** Unconscious incompetence – you are not aware that you can learn to change, and you don't know how to change.

- **Step Two:** Conscious incompetence – you are aware that change is possible, but you don't know how to implement that change.

- **Step Three:** Conscious competence – you are aware that change is possible and you are taking action, but your competency levels are not yet automatic.

- **Step Four:** Unconscious competence – you are running the new habit and behaviour all the time as an automatic response, without being aware that you are doing it.

BEFORE YOU START...

Let's bring these four steps to life, using the example of driving a car.

- **Step One:** You are not aware of how much you don't know about driving.

- **Step Two:** You start driving and become aware of the things you need to do to drive, but you have to be focused and deliberate in your actions to do all of these things and keep yourself safe.

- **Step Three:** You are now getting more and more familiar with the process of driving; it is becoming easier and feels more natural.

- **Step Four:** You are now so familiar with the process and have practised it so often that it becomes second nature, an unconscious habit of behaviour.

If you are indeed a driver, I am sure you will have had journeys where, thinking back, you don't necessarily remember it all. This is possible because you have become unconsciously competent and rely on your subconscious habits and patterns to get you to your destination safely.

My aim in this book is to get you to the level of unconscious competence in cultivating positivity so that you can enjoy living the feeling of freedom.

Harnessing the power of small incremental changes to create substantial results rather than taking massive actions is often the key to creating lasting success. Instead of attempting unsustainable actions that can lead to burnout or disappointment, focus on making consistent, gradual adjustments to behaviour. These small changes accumulate over time, bringing about meaningful and sustainable progress and becoming habits that shape our lives.

Responsibility and control

Taking responsibility is a key ingredient to profound and lasting positive change. We will all have experienced situations in life where we felt we were not in control and were not happy with our situation. It is important to acknowledge this rather than try to maintain a blindly optimistic attitude. However, taking responsibility for our reactions opens up ways for us to investigate how we can reduce the negative impact they have, both emotionally and behaviourally.

We tend to assume that we don't have control over the way we react to situations, but this is far from the truth. We have a choice, and choosing how we react is the key to having more control over the way we feel. Preparing for positive change requires us to take charge in this way; without this control, we can't guarantee the results we want.

We often underestimate the power of making an 'absolute' decision in one defining moment. Imagine drawing a line in the sand and deciding that today is the day things change. What would that do for your future?

It is easy to blame our circumstances, fate, the economy, politicians, the weather, our friends, family members or anything else outside of ourselves, but this will only result in a struggle to get a good result, as our focus is in the wrong place. It seems to have become almost fashionable to blame our parents for how we turn out as adults, but as you read and implement changes throughout the next seven days, you will discover that only one person is responsible for how you feel and behave, and that person is you.

Another thing we can be guilty of is waiting for others to change so that we can be happy. This approach results in a long wait and no results. Just imagine calling out every person who you may have blamed in the past for upsetting you, hurting you, making you angry, sad or frightened, and trying to force them to change so that you can be happy. Impossible.

You are the only person who can be responsible for your happiness. When you allow people to affect the way you feel you are essentially handing them your power. People in your life will do things that you may not like, but it is up to you to decide how you respond. While this might sound difficult now, in the next seven days, you will learn how to do so with ease.

By teaching you the methodology and practices of the Seven-Day Positivity Project, I will help you to retrieve your power, so that you can be in control of how you feel and behave.

You have all the resources you need within you to create positive change, whether you believe it or not.

The importance of community

Another wonderful and invaluable resource we have to hand is the community. We know from a large volume of peer-reviewed scientific studies that community has a huge bearing on wellness, longevity and living happier lives.[3,4,5]

Having grown a strong community around the Seven-Day Positivity Project I have witnessed for myself the positive effects it has on wellbeing, quality of life and levels of happiness. One of the most treasured statements in our community is 'stay in the circle'. Sometimes we may not feel like it, but even reading just one page of this book or applying a single technique will be beneficial.

This is why I strongly encourage you to seek out and participate in a community to support your positivity journey. After your first read-though of this book and once you are committed to change, I recommend you start Day One again and repeat the process of working through the seven days. You don't need to go it alone; you can join our community to engage with likeminded people and feel supported on your journey by visiting www.moirageary.com/community and requesting to join.

Positive psychology

Much of the Seven-Day Positivity Project draws on elements of positive psychology, so it is important to have some understanding of its theoretical underpinnings as we begin our journey.

Positive psychology is an area of science that concentrates on cultivating and understanding human strengths and qualities, rather than analysing and addressing mental illness. It identifies and encourages conditions that foster wellbeing, resilience and flourishing. Positive psychology will help you to enhance positive emotions, engage in fulfilling activities, build positive relationships and find meaning and purpose in life. Focusing on the positive aspects of human nature helps people to realise their full potential and leads to happier, more rewarding lives.[6,7,8]

Positive thinking is a fabulous approach, as it focuses the mind on solutions, possibilities and potential outcomes, all of which are necessary for achieving positive results. However, there is also an element of positive thinking commonly referred to as 'toxic positivity', which can be harmful. Toxic positivity is trying to maintain a positive attitude *all* the time, even in difficult or negative situations. This can show up as downplaying or dismissing negative emotions or experiences, or pressuring others to always think positively.

While it's important to have a positive outlook on life and to try to find the good in difficult situations, toxic positivity can be harmful in three main ways:

1. It can invalidate people's genuine feelings and experiences.

2. It can create an unhealthy pressure to always be positive, which can be emotionally exhausting and unsustainable.

3. It can prevent people from looking for help or support when they need it.

Nevertheless, when used correctly, positive psychology and thinking are powerful tools. Adopting a more positive outlook and focusing on positive thoughts is beneficial for our mental health.

Summary

This book aims to help you create sustainable positive change in your life, and positive psychology offers powerful tools for doing so. You can start the process of embedding new habits, patterns of behaviour and skills by absorbing the information in this

BEFORE YOU START...

book and implementing it daily. To set yourself up for success, bear in mind the following as you get started:

- Bringing about lasting, effective behavioural and emotional change does not have to be difficult or time-consuming.

- Don't underestimate the importance of habits and the impact they have on your behaviour and feelings. If they're not serving you well, you can change them.

- Making small incremental changes will have an effect that compounds over time.

- Taking responsibility for your reactions to situations is crucial for creating positive change.

TWO
Day One: The Power Of Your Mind

In this chapter, I will introduce you to the conscious and subconscious minds and the way they influence how we behave and feel, as well as the RAS. This opens up the topic of how we interpret information and use that interpretation to shape our behaviours, motivations and the results we get in life.

The mind is one of our biggest mysteries. What is it? It is easy to think about and understand the brain: it is an organ housed in our skull; it is tangible, it has parts and structure and, to a degree, we understand some of its functioning. However, our mind is not tangible; we can't see it or hold it, and we don't know *where* it exists. Yet we know that it does, through our perceptions, our thinking, desires, sensations, memories, beliefs and emotions. Even though the learnings to date in this area are limited, we do have enough understanding of the mind to use some of our knowledge of its functioning to enhance our lives.

The first thing to note is that the subconscious and conscious minds are not two separate minds but two parts of one mind, and it is important for your happiness that they work together and support each other. The following explanation is by no means comprehensive, but it will help you to understand the foundations of the Positivity Project.

Your conscious mind

The analogy of a computer is useful to explain the two parts of the mind and how they function. In this analogy, the screen and the keyboard of the computer represent your conscious mind, and the hard drive represents your subconscious mind.

When you consider the processing capability of a computer, the hardware is responsible for about 5–10% of the processing capability, whereas the hard drive accounts for the other 90–95%. The same is true for your conscious and subconscious minds. Your conscious mind is responsible for just a tiny portion of the processing capability of your mind, and your subconscious mind is responsible for much more than we previously thought.[9,10]

Having said that, your conscious mind can act as the conduit for what goes into your subconscious mind by letting information in. When you are aware of this, you can be selective about what you focus on in life and allow it to filter through.

Your conscious conduit

In its role as a conduit or channel, the conscious mind can filter the information that goes through to the subconscious mind to allow only empowering and positive messages. Most people do not realise the importance of the work of the conscious mind, and they are unaware that they're not using it to their best advantage. If we are aware of this, we can take control and start to prevent negative and disempowering suggestions from penetrating the subconscious mind.

Many of us may not be aware of the extent to which we allow ourselves to become socially hypnotised and negatively influenced by the media, religious and educational institutions, politicians, family members, peers and so forth. If there were no repercussions from receiving these negative suggestions at the subconscious level, this would not be a problem. Unfortunately, there are many.

What the conscious mind controls

Your conscious mind is in charge of reasoning, decision-making, working out pros and cons, and willpower. It is your objective, logical mind. It processes the information received through your sensory filters giving it meaning.

You are exposed to thousands of pieces of information every second; you need to filter this information to avoid total overwhelm. You do this through what you see, hear, smell, taste and touch, but you also can delete, distort and generalise information, depending on your needs. This greatly reduces the amount that gets through to the subconscious mind, with only the most important information making it through.

The conscious mind is also the leader; it gives instructions to the subconscious mind on how to behave or respond to situations.

But most of us, at times, allow our conscious mind to nod off. In this state of unawareness, it does a bad job of guarding the subconscious mind from disempowering suggestions that come from external sources.

When we experience situations, our conscious mind can also make poor judgements about what actually happened, choosing to find a disempowering meaning and labelling them as 'bad experiences'. This can create negative and limiting beliefs, which have a direct impact on what we achieve in our lives.

Your subconscious mind

The difference between people who are fearful, sad, full of doubt, constantly struggling, overwhelmed and unhappy, and people who are successful, confident and joyful is influenced by the workings of the subconscious mind. Once we understand this and can access the tools to help us master the power of our subconscious mind, our lives will quickly change for the better.

At birth, the subconscious mind is empty of memories, beliefs and values because we have not yet had any life experiences. As soon as we begin to live, it starts to fill up.

The subconscious mind, just like a hard drive, is great at storing information and then running whichever programmes are installed. If your conscious mind is not alert and on guard, it will allow negative information and suggestions to slip down to the subconscious level. The subconscious mind can only be expected to do what it does best: efficiently operating as instructed by the conscious mind. That means it will run and repeat whatever programmes it is given – positive or negative – for as long as they remain installed.

Your protector

One of the primary functions of your subconscious mind is to protect you, both physically and emotionally. In this book, we are more interested in emotional protection but let me just briefly explain how it protects you physically.

How many times today have you consciously reminded yourself to blink? I am sure that for most (if not all) of you, the answer is not once. How many times today have you consciously reminded yourself to breathe? Again, I'm sure for most the answer would be not once.

But we have to breathe and blink to stay alive and comfortable. Even though you are not consciously aware that you are blinking every few seconds or breathing twenty or so times every minute, your subconscious mind knows what needs to be done and is taking care of that for you.

Think about how many times you might have consciously driven a car. Can you remember consciously giving yourself instructions to change the gears, put the indicators on or turn the steering wheel during the journey? If it wasn't your conscious mind driving the car, then what was? Yes: your subconscious mind.

Imagine you were driving and someone ran out onto the road in front of you. Would you rely on your conscious mind to say, 'Oh, someone is running out in front of me onto the road, I had better put my foot on the brake and stop the car'? Of course not. That conscious instruction is too slow. Again, you are relying on your subconscious mind to keep you (and everyone else) safe. It will automatically make you jam on the brakes and stop the car before your conscious mind is even aware of what is happening.

That's how your subconscious protects you physically, but the emotional protection it provides is where it gets exciting. Your subconscious mind is always striving to make you feel safe and happy, twenty-four hours a day, seven days a week.

When we are born, our subconscious mind is hard-wired with a default programme that supports our need for survival and happiness. This programming will be explained in more detail later in the book when we discuss the Seven Behavioural Codes®. For now, let's have a look at the general concept of how the subconscious mind does its best to protect us emotionally.

Memories

Everything you have ever experienced is stored in the memory compartment of the hard drive of the computer of your mind: your subconscious.

Every time you think or experience something, you filter that information through your five senses. Your conscious and subconscious minds then delete some of the unnecessary information, distort some of it to make better sense of it, and generalise some of it to make it easy for you to compute. Once that's all done, the memory of the thought or experience is stored in your subconscious mind. However, how does this protect you, or help you to feel happy?

Well, as you experience situations, you also feel something about them. In many cases, this may be a relaxed, bland or even bored feeling, but when you experience a situation that has a significant emotional charge, your feelings are at a higher intensity.

As well as your experiences and memories, your subconscious mind also creates and embeds a neurological pathway for the emotions you were feeling in those moments and how you felt physically. Physical and emotional feelings are closely linked and are subconsciously connected. An excited feeling might be linked to the physical feeling of butterflies in your tummy; a sad feeling might correlate to the physical feeling of a lump in your throat or a heaviness in your chest.

The feelings associated with memories of significant emotional events will be more intense, as these trigger strong emotional responses. These can be positive or negative.

In its role as protector, the subconscious mind will recreate the bad feelings associated with negative memories at a higher intensity than it does for positive ones. If you are exposed to a similar situation in the future, the subconscious mind will reactivate the neurological pathway of the negative feeling related to that particular event or memory, which will make you feel physically uncomfortable, in a bid to alert you of the potential danger.[11,12,13] You might think that protecting a person by making them feel bad is a bit strange, but actually, it is a highly effective way – once bitten, twice shy. Where it perceives potential for you to feel bad again in the future, your subconscious mind will reactivate that negative feeling to warn you of that situation, thus protecting you. Remember, the subconscious mind doesn't discriminate. It simply acts as it's programmed to.

Public speaking is a common example of this mechanism in action, as the below story highlights.

CASE STUDY: Emmet's story

When Emmet, a client of mine, was a small boy, he was full of confidence and enthusiasm. Getting up and singing in front of people or reciting a poem was effortless. Unfortunately, it only took one experience, when he willingly stood up to answer a question in school and was ridiculed by his peers, for him to feel shame and a sense of not being good enough. His subconscious mind created a neurological pathway associated with the memory of this experience and the uncomfortable feeling in his body.

Even the anticipation of speaking in front of people was enough for his subconscious mind to access the memory and reactivate that feeling of discomfort.

His subconscious mind was doing a great job of 'protecting' him by warning him through fear.

We addressed this by using the Problem Not Problem® technique, as well as the power of language, to try and reduce the fear and make the subconscious pattern redundant. We followed this with empowerment coaching and taking inspired action. He has now regained his confidence and no longer experiences this fear and physical discomfort when speaking in public.

This is just one example of hundreds of similar client stories. Many of these clients recreated the situations so vividly in their minds that they often resulted in full-blown panic attacks.

Chin up – why physiology matters

Now that we understand some of the workings of our mind, it's time to look at the influence of our physiology and how it impacts the way we feel and behave. The statement 'Chin up!' for some can be a trigger, as they may have heard it as a child from parents, grandparents or other caregivers as an instruction to cheer up or to pull themselves out of a funk. This can be upsetting, suggesting that our emotions are not valid. However, we can repurpose the phrase for good and see that there is great wisdom in this statement if we understand it in a different, more literal way.

When we follow the instruction 'chin up' and raise our chin from having it dropped or close to our chest to a position where we can look straight ahead, or even slightly upwards, we start to change our physiology – which has the power to change how we feel on the inside.

Human physiology is heavily influenced by our tendency to focus on negative information more than positive information, a phenomenon known as negativity bias.[14,15] When experiencing negativity bias about what might be going on in our lives, we also tend to feel a corresponding negative emotion – we might feel stressed, overwhelmed and anxious. In this way, we are subconsciously trying to protect ourselves by focusing on what might go wrong so that we are aware and alert to the need to make changes to prevent or avoid potential negative outcomes.

One way we make sense of information is to first talk to ourselves – in our heads. Any negative talk will, in turn, conjure up a corresponding emotion and physical feeling in our bodies, bringing us into an overall stressed state. At the same time, our stance changes, and we end up in a 'closed physiology', which is what we tend to display when feeling low or depressed.[16] A closed physiology is characterised by slouched, rounded shoulders and a drooping head. It is usually accessorised with a matching internal running commentary about everything that could go wrong, all that we are worried about, our biggest fears for ourselves, our families, our jobs and our situations. All of you who have experienced this will know exactly what I mean. However, once you are aware of it, you have the power to make changes to avoid this debilitating state.

The opposite of a closed physiology is an open physiology, which is identified as a posture with an erect spine, shoulders open and chin up. From my personal experience and my experience with clients, raising your gaze and looking up to the ceiling or sky also increases the effectiveness of the 'chin up' stance. Holding this open posture gives rise to feelings of alertness, confidence, excitation and satisfaction. Reminding yourself to 'chin up' and acting on it several times during the day will instantly change your state of being, how you feel and what you are saying to yourself in your head.

To help you experience this for yourself, below is a short and effective exercise to demonstrate the concept.

EXERCISE: Chin up

For you to feel the benefit of the exercise, you first need to sit or stand with a closed physiology:

- Round your shoulders.
- Drop your head with your chin towards your chest.
- Put a frown on your face.
- Drop your gaze down towards the floor.
- Think of something that is not going so well in your world.
- Engage in internal dialogue about that subject.

DAY ONE: THE POWER OF YOUR MIND

Once you are doing all of those things, notice how you are feeling emotionally. How low or high is your mood? Give this feeling a score on a scale of one to ten.

Now it's time to change your physiology:

- Stand or sit erect.
- Open your shoulders.
- Raise your chin.
- Raise your gaze toward the ceiling.
- Replace your frown with a big smile.

Hold that physiology, and now I want you to try with every cell in your body to feel bad. If you are doing the exercise at 100%, you'll notice it is impossible. Now measure on a scale of one to ten how you are feeling and compare this to your initial measurement from your closed physiology. Notice what is different and acknowledge it.

You can do this exercise immediately after getting out of bed in the morning, while on a walk, taking a few minutes out for a cuppa, waiting in the car for someone, before going to an appointment, while brushing your teeth or in any other moments when you're alone.

The benefits are numerous and include increasing your feelings of positive personal autonomy, improving emotional self-regulation, reducing stress and elevating your mood – generally feeling good on the inside.

Gratitude

Our second concept for today is gratitude. This may not be a new concept to you, but there are many proven approaches to the subject supported by research; understanding these and applying them can enhance your life. You may have already used a gratitude journal. If you have, that's great, but for those of you who haven't or who may be sceptical, let's break the practice down so that we can understand why gratitude exercises have so many benefits in reducing stress, boosting self-esteem and increasing overall satisfaction with life.

Most people engaging in gratitude practices are inclined to keep things general, by which I mean that they keep a journal with entries like: 'I am grateful for my home, my family, my friends' etc. This is not wrong or bad *per se* and can elicit some of the many positive effects of feeling gratitude. However, when we get more specific, engaging the mind in accessing more detail, this enhances the feeling of gratitude, which increases the benefits of the gratitude practice. These benefits include enhanced wellbeing, better quality sleep and reduced incidence of depression.[17]

Below is an easy daily exercise to help you get more specific with your gratitude practice

> **EXERCISE: Recording gratitude**
>
> Decide on a time that you will do your daily gratitude practice. I want you to write down your gratitude notes rather than typing them out or just thinking about them; writing will have a deeper and more positive effect. The practice itself is simple:
>
> - Write no more than three things you are grateful for that day.
> - Then take each of these things in turn and think of three reasons why you are grateful for them.
>
> Over the years, my clients have consistently reported deeper positive results from adding the question of why they are grateful for something to the exercise. Going deeper into the reasons why allows them to evoke, and connect with, a deeper, more visceral feeling of gratitude in their physical body, increasing the benefits of the practice. Remember, positive psychology is about flourishing and thriving; this simple practice of gratitude supports exactly that.

With the Positivity Project, I am focused on helping you understand why it is beneficial to do these practices, but it is up to you to consistently apply them.

Prime yourself

There is also a whole other reason to do gratitude exercises. When we focus on what we are grateful for, we are subconsciously saying that we are abundant in some way. It then follows that we will viscerally feel that abundance in our physical body. This activates and primes the RAS to seek out and focus on ways to bring more abundance into our lives, which is extremely beneficial in times when we are feeling disillusioned or a bit low.

To explain further, the RAS is a survival mechanism. It is comprised of a collection of nerves situated in the brainstem, and part of its role is to regulate our behaviour and motivation.[18,19] In simple terms, the RAS filters information coming into our brain which can influence our motivations for behaviours. It is like the interface between the information your senses experience – ie, what you see, hear, smell, taste and touch in the world – and how you filter that information to create an interpretation of your reality.

A simple example of the RAS at work is what happens when you buy a new car. You decide on the make, model and possibly even the colour you are looking to purchase. Then, as you are going about day to day, you notice that you are seeing those cars, which were not previously in your conscious awareness, everywhere. Your RAS was primed when you decided on the car, and it is now helping you to notice what you want. As your RAS influences behaviour and motivation, it can also guide you to seek out and implement a strategy to attain the car.

Positive expectations

Our third concept for today follows on from the focus on gratitude. It is the practice of focusing on positive expectations. This also engages the RAS. Focusing on positive expectations means putting our attention on the expectation that things in our life will work out, or go the way we want them to, rather than ruminating on everything that could go wrong. I am not asking you to implement this concept twenty-four seven, but rather to start with becoming aware, perhaps just once an hour for a few days, of where you are focusing or placing your attention in terms of positive or negative expectations. By priming your subconscious mind to expect good things to happen, it is more likely to notice opportunities for you to *make* them happen, thus enhancing your life.

I am not saying that good things will always happen in life if you expect or want them to – life has a habit of giving us the rough end of the pineapple from time to time, and it does throw us curve balls. However, by knowing and implementing this technique, you have a better chance of finding more joy and positivity in your life and of increasing your ability to do the best you can with what you have. The exercise below is a great place to get started with shifting your focus to a more positive place.

> **EXERCISE: Positive expectation**
>
> To do this exercise, I suggest you use some form of (subtle) alarm on your phone that will chime on the hour. Many apps can do this.
>
> - When you hear the chime, become aware of where your focus was for the majority of the previous hour about your expectations. Were they positive or negative? It is important not to judge yourself if your focus is not where you would like it to be. The aim is just to become aware.
> - Now that you have a baseline for your 'expectation' focus, work on increasing the amount of time you focus on positive expectations.
> - When you hear the next chime and have checked in on your focus, make a conscious effort to put more focus on positive expectations for the next hour.
>
> Like learning or creating any new habit, this takes a little time and consistency, but it's worth it for the benefits you will gain in how you feel on a moment-to-moment basis. For an extra supercharge you can also keep track of your progress in a journal.

Summary

The power of our minds is, for many, an untapped resource. Developing an understanding of how you can use that power is key to your progress towards positivity:

- Start harnessing your subconscious to improve your life.

- Remembering to 'Chin up!' can instantly life your mood.

- Creating a detailed picture of all that you are grateful for can enhance your sleep, mood and overall wellbeing.

- Focusing on positive expectations primes you to notice all the positive elements in your life.

- Writing things down can help you see your progress and support better and sustained results.

THREE
Day Two: Take Control

Most of us, when we are thinking of an experience, either from the past or one we are anticipating, create images in our minds to help us compute it. The images can range from being vague and out of focus to vivid and crystal clear. However, the important component – the one that increases or decreases the emotional intensity of the image – is whether we can see ourselves in the picture or not; whether we are associated into it or dissociated from it.

Association/disassociation

Understanding association and disassociation is essential for getting the best out of the exercises I'll introduce as we progress through the project, because these concepts can help us increase or decrease the emotional intensity of our experiences. If we can see ourselves in the image, we are distancing ourselves from the experience in our minds and are therefore disassociated. When we are associated into the experience, we are *inside* the image or thought. We are wholly immersed in it, looking out through our own eyes, seeing what we would see, hearing what we would hear, and feeling a deep sense of what it would be like to have that experience.

When we wish to intensify the feeling attached to any image or thought, we must associate ourselves into the image so that we can't see ourselves in it. The opposite is also true: if we want to reduce the intensity of the feeling attached to an image, we must disassociate ourselves from the image in our thought, by looking from the 'outside' at ourselves in the picture of that experience or situation. In many of the forthcoming exercises, I'll guide you to associate or disassociate when appropriate, to increase helpful feelings and reduce unhelpful ones.

The kind of language used to help people associate includes:

- 'As you bring the memory closer to you...'
- 'As you step into that memory...'
- 'While you are in that memory, see what you will see, hear what you will hear and feel what you will feel...'

DAY TWO: TAKE CONTROL

Language used to help people disassociate includes:

- 'As you step back from/out of the memory…'
- 'Now float out of yourself in the memory and notice how you can see yourself from a distance…'
- 'Notice how you can observe yourself in the memory…'

> **EXERCISE: Finding your baseline**
>
> Throughout this project, you will want to measure your progress. To do this, you need to get a baseline of where you are now. I suggest doing this for many of the exercises in the project: find your baseline and then use it to consciously embed new practices to build your better future.
>
> Use a device that has the facility to sound an alarm every hour. For example, you could download an app that will chime at the intervals you select (as in the previous exercise). After you've decided on the exercise you want to do and you've set your alarm for hourly intervals, prime yourself to notice what is your norm for this exercise during that hour. Don't bring in any judgement, just notice. If you notice you were displaying the habit for 1% of the hour, that is your baseline. You can decide to try and increase that by a certain percentage for the next hour. Bringing your awareness to the exercise and the

> habit in question on an hourly basis for a few days will help prime your subconscious mind to take over and establish the new, empowering, way of doing things.

Mind–body connection

As we've learned, how we think impacts how we feel, which in turn impacts the physiological workings of our body. We've also established that we can increase or decrease the feelings related to a thought when we decide to associate into or disassociate ourselves from that thought.

When we think stressful or fear-related thoughts, and we are associated into those thoughts, our endocrine system secretes the stress hormones cortisol and adrenaline into our bloodstream, setting up a stress response in our bodies.[20,21] The physical symptoms of the stress response include butterflies in the tummy, dry mouth and an increased heart rate. The same is true if you focus on happy and pleasing thoughts and images: this will stimulate the secretion of hormones like endorphins, oxytocin, serotonin and dopamine, which give us feelings of joy, love and bliss.

The exercise below will enable you to experience this mind–body connection without triggering a stress response.

> **EXERCISE: Tasting an imaginary lemon**
>
> Follow the steps below:
>
> - With your eyes closed, imagine a bright yellow lemon and a sharp knife on a chopping board in front of you.
> - Imagine picking up the knife and easily slicing the lemon in half, noticing how ripe and juicy it is.
> - Next, imagine yourself picking up half of the lemon and, with your head tilted back, your mouth open and your tongue raised, squeezing the juice from the lemon under your tongue.
> - Now notice how your mouth is producing saliva, even though there is no lemon – you have just imagined it.

The above exercise shows how we can have a clear, strong physiological reaction to a thought and an internal image that we are associated into. Now imagine how often this happens during your day. Our exercise related to a neutral image. However, what if it is happening with stressful thoughts and worrying images of things that will never happen? This can have a negative effect on you, physically and emotionally.

> **EXERCISE: Positive thinking**
>
> This exercise will help to counteract automatic stressful thoughts, to avoid their negative effects.

- First thing in the morning, decide to think positively for the day.
- Associate into thoughts and images that will have a soothing and uplifting effect on you, physically and emotionally. Put yourself inside the thought, looking out through your eyes, seeing what you would see, hearing what you would hear, feeling the feelings of being in that positive thought – and enjoy it.
- Use your hourly chime to remind yourself of this decision for seven days.

Remember that using the hourly alarm allows you to establish a baseline of where you naturally focus your thoughts. Do this with compassion for yourself and no judgement. When you have established your baseline, set an intention to increase the time you are focusing on thoughts that support you. In time, with practice, there will come a tipping point where you will have conditioned yourself to focus mainly on supporting thoughts and images rather than on negative ones. Bear in mind that this is not a linear process, and you may relapse in some of the hours, but just notice it and move on.

Managing problems

All of us experience problems in one form or another – they are part of life and we can learn a great deal from solving, overcoming and managing them. However, for some they can create havoc, often leaving people with a sense of hopelessness, worry, stress, fear and overwhelm. It is important to acknowledge that a problem exists; we do not want to sweep it under the carpet.

We saw on Day One how a primary function of the subconscious mind is to protect us emotionally. When we have a problem and feel stressed because it has not yet been resolved, our subconscious can fixate on the problem, trying to solve it so that we can feel relief from our worries. However, we are usually associated into this fixation. It's like covering our eyes with the problem so that it's all we can see. Yet we know that when we associate into something, the feelings it is causing intensify, giving rise to more stress and overwhelm.

To effectively problem-solve, you need to be in a state of calm, so that you can think clearly, quantify the problem and come up with an effective solution. The 'problem not problem' exercise below will help you to do this. In it, we are acknowledging that a problem exists, then taking specific steps to feel less stressed and overwhelmed by it, and formulating a plan to solve it.

> **EXERCISE: Problem not problem**
>
> To prepare for the exercise, identify one problem in your life that may be overtaking your thinking and causing stress. If you don't currently have a problem like this, think of one you had in the past. Use an object like a piece of card or paper about 10 cm in diameter to represent your problem.

I have a black circle cut-out in my office that I regularly use for this exercise. For now, if you don't have a suitable object, you can use your hand.

- As you think about the problem, notice how it becomes all-consuming and how you become associated into the scenario, starting to experience feelings linked to the problem.
- Take note on a scale of one to ten how intense the feelings related to the problem are when you are totally associated into it.
- With your eyes open, place your object or your hand in front of your eyes and touch your face with it.
- Notice that when the object representing your problem is in front of your eyes, you are not able to see anything else.
- Become aware that the solution to any problem does not lie in the problem itself but outside of it; continuing to look only at the problem and being associated into it will only maintain the stress and overwhelm.
- Start to move the object away from your eyes and out in front of you, disassociating yourself from it. If you can, stick the object on a wall in front of you, anywhere from ten to fifteen feet away or more.
- As you step back from it, take note of how the feelings of stress and overwhelm have reduced, and of your increased ability to think straight once you have disassociated from the problem.

DAY TWO: TAKE CONTROL

- Now that the problem is on the wall in front of you, become aware of its size in relation to everything else and acknowledge it as simply something that needs to be solved.
- Remind yourself that the solution to the problem is not *in* the problem. The solution is in the 'not problem'. The 'not problem' is everywhere else outside of the black dot on the wall, meaning the room, the building, the county, state, country, continent, planet, universe...
- Notice how the feelings related to the problem have reduced further.
- Now ask yourself two questions: 'In the history of the universe, has anyone ever solved this problem or a similar problem?' 'What did they do to solve it that I can also do?'
- Make notes of the solutions that are coming to you.

You may need to come back to this a few times over the coming days/weeks to consolidate the solution and the steps you need to take, but all the while you will be feeling less stressed about and overwhelmed by your problem.

Golden Rule 1: Change your perception of reality

As the final topic of Day Two, I am sharing our first Golden Rule. It relates to the fact that it is easier to make changes within ourselves and to our perception of reality than to try and change other people and situations. When we decide to look at the world differently, it promotes imagination and offers up possibilities and opportunities that we may not see if we stay focused on a difficult situation that exists outside of us.

I often see unhappy people who believe that if only the people or circumstances around them would change, they would be happy. This is the wrong attitude when we are looking to increase our happiness, joy and peace of mind. Trying to force others to behave differently so that you can be happy will leave you furious, exhausted and stressed.

Why? Because people don't want to change their behaviours to make you happy – they are too busy trying to make themselves happy. Changing your perception of your reality is a much easier, quicker and more reliable route to happiness, as the below story illustrates.

CASE STUDY: Christine's story

An eighteen-year-old client of mine called Christine came to me about the severe panic she was experiencing when walking into school. It was her final year – an important time, as her exam results would map out her college years and beyond.

When she first arrived, I thought we would be looking at exam stress, but her behavioural pattern turned out to be focused on something completely different. It had been created and embedded in her subconscious long before she ever started school. When she was three, her father left home one day without warning and didn't come back.

Christine had had no communication with him since he'd left. That three-year-old Christine unknowingly set up a subconscious pattern on that day, one that signalled for her that the world is unsafe and life can change in an instant without warning. This pattern was then reinforced by a move to a new city seven years later when she had to part with family and close friends again.

Christine was having panic attacks in her final year of school because the stress of the exams was triggering a much deeper fear of separation and of the insecurity of her world, which she had been suppressing for years. She was not aware of this pattern as, to protect her, her subconscious mind had not allowed her to revisit the memories.

We worked on introducing the first Golden Rule and started to change her perception of her reality through our coaching sessions. We followed this by challenging her perception of her reality (we'll reach this on day five of the project), which interrupted her internal subconscious pattern. This began to gently release her fears and, after two sessions, she was able to return to school without fear or panic.

In the story above, if we had decided to manage Christine's situation by trying to change all the things outside of her that related to the problem of not being able to walk into school without panic, we would have had quite the task. Instead, I helped her to change her perception of her reality, rather than trying to change the circumstances. In other words, we changed the way she was looking at and responding to the experience of walking into school rather than attempting to change the teachers, students and the dynamics of the school. This approach is a lot easier and much more effective and the results are long lasting.

Summary

We don't need to be held captive by our thoughts and emotions. There are many ways in which we can take control of our thinking and manage our emotions:

- Once we understand how association and disassociation support the increase or decrease in the emotional intensity of our experiences, we can use this to control our thoughts and images, focusing on those that will promote our wellbeing.

- The mind–body connection is evident in how our thoughts impact how we feel, which affects the physiological workings of our body. We can cause stress or joy, depending on the type of thoughts and images we focus on.

- To help counteract negative thinking, associate yourself into positive thoughts and images for a day, using an hourly alarm for support.

- Use the 'Problem not problem' exercise to help manage your state of mind when you face a problem situation. This will promote a practical approach to finding solutions.

- It is usually easier to change your perception of reality than to try to change your external circumstances.

FOUR
Day Three: Order Out Of Chaos

Everyone on the planet experiences feelings and emotions every day, and that serves us well. Our feelings, whether or not we are aware of them, will dictate our behaviour. When you take action or respond to something in a particular way, the process always involves your subconscious mind first deciding on the behaviour in a bid to make you feel good and to keep you safe in some way.

Fear

Fear is one of the most powerful human emotions. It arises in response to perceived threats or dangers and is an innate survival mechanism that helps to protect us from potential harm. When we experience fear, our minds and bodies go into a heightened feeling of alertness, preparing us to either confront the threat or run from it – fight or flight.

If you feel an intense fear of public speaking, for example, you are likely to avoid it at all costs, unless you are willing to feel the fear deeply and push through it. Your subconscious will be screaming at you not to do it because you might make a mistake and feel shame and embarrassment, or be rejected by your audience. Those who have had positive experiences speaking in public in the past and felt confident, strong and empowered as a result, are more likely to embrace it, in a bid to recreate those positive feelings for themselves and others.

The experience of fear involves a complex interplay between our thoughts, emotions and the physiological responses in our bodies. It begins with the perception of a threat, which can be real or imagined, physical or emotional. In this book, the emotional threat is our main focus. This perceived threat triggers a cascade of reactions, starting in our brains – particularly in the amygdala, which is responsible for processing emotions and initiating the 'fight or flight' response.[22]

Fear can be triggered by various things – physical danger, traumatic experiences, phobias, social situations or even abstract concepts, like a fear of the unknown. It can be experienced in different intensities, ranging from mild uneasiness to intense terror.

Acknowledging it is the first step to managing it; we need to familiarise ourselves with where we physically feel the fear in our bodies. Usually, it will be in the pit of your tummy, mid-tummy, solar plexus (just under the breastbone), in your heart area or throat.

As mentioned, fear activates the sympathetic nervous system, leading to a surge of stress hormones, namely adrenaline and cortisol. These hormones increase heart rate, blood pressure and respiration while redirecting blood flow to the muscles to enhance strength and speed. This physiological response primes the body for action, enabling us to either confront the threat (fight) or escape from it (flight). It is often accompanied by a sense of dread, anxiety or panic.

Fear can have both short-term and long-term effects on wellbeing, and is not always a 'bad' thing. In the short term, fear can help us to react quickly and protect ourselves from immediate dangers. However, fear that is prolonged, excessive or disproportionate to the circumstances can be detrimental to our physical, mental and emotional health, leading to chronic stress and anxiety.

Understanding and managing fear is an important aspect of living a more positive life and enjoying emotional wellbeing. By acknowledging and addressing our fears, we develop resilience and confidence. One of the most common and stressful modes of fear – one that stops us from experiencing mental and emotional freedom – is worry.

The process of worry

Worry involves a preoccupation with a possible future event or circumstance. The process of worrying involves several stages, from the perception of a potential threat – that is, how we imagine things going wrong – to the physiological and emotional responses we then feel in our bodies. Let's walk through the process to better understand it.

Below is the sequence of thoughts and responses we may experience when we worry about something that may or may not happen:

- We perceive a threat. This could be a real and immediate threat, such as a meeting you need to present at tomorrow, or an imagined threat, such as worrying without reason that something might happen to a friend or family member.

- As a result of perceiving the threat, the brain's fear response is activated in the amygdala, a region of the brain responsible for processing emotions. The amygdala quickly evaluates the potential threat and triggers a series of responses.

- The first of these responses is fight or flight, which prepares us to either confront the threat or escape from it. This involves the release of adrenaline and cortisol into the bloodstream.

- The resulting physiological changes include increased heart rate, raised blood pressure, rapid breathing, tensed muscles and heightened senses. Blood flow is directed away from non-essential functions like digestion and towards the muscles, to enhance strength and agility.

- Then the emotional experience of fear kicks in. This can include feelings of anxiety, apprehension, panic or terror. The emotional response to fear varies depending on the intensity and context of the perceived threat.

- Finally, the cognitive or thought reaction is activated: the mind may become focused on the perceived threat, leading to narrowed attention and heightened vigilance (as described in the 'Problem not problem' exercise from Day Two). This can generate negative thoughts and catastrophic thinking, where we imagine the worst possible outcomes associated with the threat.

At this point, if we control the focus of our thoughts, we can reduce the fear. We assume that what we are afraid of is the thing that might happen – losing our job, making a major mistake at work, our child getting hurt etc. However, we are not actually afraid of those things happening; what we are actually afraid of is, first of all, the uncertainty of not knowing whether or not the thing *will* happen and, second, how will we cope if it does.

To reduce worry, fear and stress, it can help to take a little time to think about how we would cope in certain situations. This calms the fear response, as our subconscious mind now knows we have a plan or ways of managing.

CASE STUDY: Joe's story

I often recount (with permission) the story of my eldest son, Joe, and his love of Parkour – a sport involving vaulting, climbing and jumping substantial heights to get from one point to another. Even though he was good at it, as his mother I was afraid that he might have an accident. My fears were realised one day when he wasn't even doing Parkour but was climbing a castle ruin. He fell 30 feet and sustained a severe head wound. I remember, as my husband and I waited in the hospital for the doctor to give us the results of his X-rays and tests, the feeling of not knowing what his injuries could mean for him and us as a family. I was going through all the possible scenarios in my head of what might happen and how we would cope. This was a deep lesson for me in how my real fear was not so much of Joe having an accident, but of the unknown, the uncertainty as to how we would cope depending on the outcome. (Thankfully, Joe's injuries were confined to open head wounds and cuts and bruises, without any neurological damage.)

Of course, the process of worry will vary from person to person and is influenced by individual differences, past experiences and cultural factors. Some individuals may have heightened or more frequent worry responses, while others may have different coping mechanisms or ways of regulating fear.

Overwhelm

Overwhelm is a hugely painful and disempowering state when you are trying to move forward in life. It can stop you from progressing in any situation or aspect of your life and leave you feeling like you are not in control. If you don't understand overwhelm or don't know how to deal with it, it can cripple you.

Overwhelm arises when we have several things going on in our lives and we allow the thoughts produced by these situations to inhabit space in our minds. If you start your day by thinking, 'How am I going to get the children ready for school on time and not be late for work? Oh, work. I forgot that I didn't finish that project last night. Oh, no. I need to present it today at 11am. That reminds me, I was meant to ring Mum last night. I wonder how she is after yesterday? Oh, the dog… I must do something about those vaccinations. I need a holiday. Wasn't John supposed to tell me which dates he is free to go away? If he doesn't tell me soon there will be no holiday. I wish I didn't have this back pain. Work project. Yes, work project…

how will I get it done? Oh – I forgot to check who is collecting the children from school today, I had better do that now...' and so it goes on.

The best way for me to describe overwhelm is as a swirling of different thoughts going around in your head, a bit like a washing machine. The thoughts are spinning fast, they concern many subjects and they are all mixed up together. As a result, it is difficult to organise or even make sense of them. However, without an organisation of your thoughts, the actions you take will also be disorganised, incomplete and confused, leading to further feelings of stress, overwhelm and lack of control.

When we have a lot of different things going on in our lives (despite all the gadgets and machines that help us to save time and be organised), we push ourselves and put ourselves under pressure with deadlines and goals. To reach these deadlines and achieve these goals, we often juggle thoughts about all the different subjects and agendas simultaneously. If we add enough subjects and thoughts, our conscious and subconscious minds cannot make sense of them, so they just go around in a loop. We are confused; we are unable to decide because there is no order; and our results suffer, as does our peace of mind.

Let's do something about that, starting with the below exercise.

EXERCISE: Get your head straight

I created this technique to help relieve overwhelm. You can use it at any time that you feel you need it, following the steps below:

- Consciously instruct the washing machine in your head to slow down, even bring it to a stop.
- Group the thoughts that are causing you overwhelm into subjects. These are easy to find when you look at the thoughts you have been having. Examples include work, domestic tasks, children, study, health and finances.
- Get a separate sheet of paper for each subject and write down all the thoughts you've been having about each subject. This includes things you need to do, things that are already complete or things you are concerned about. Notice how much calmer your mind feels once they are out of your head and on paper.
- Remind yourself to keep them there.
- Now decide which subject you want to focus on, safe in the knowledge that the other subjects are on a separate sheet of paper and won't be forgotten.
- Focus on the subject you've chosen and give it your full attention. This singular focus will accelerate and enhance your results or achievements.
- Consciously remind yourself that all your thoughts will stay on the paper. When you need them again they will be there; you do not need to put them back in your head.

> This is a much better way to approach a problem or task, giving you clarity and focus in place of overwhelm.

I used the above technique with a client who was training to be a helicopter pilot. As you can imagine, there is no place for overwhelm in the cockpit. Read his story below.

CASE STUDY: Gerry's story

Gerry started his journey to becoming a helicopter pilot in Ireland, where air traffic is rather less manic than in other parts of the world. In the quest for his pilot's licence, Gerry had to attend training and undergo examinations in the UK, where the skies would be much busier.

During his in-flight examination, Gerry was to receive instructions from air traffic control. These would increase from one to two instructions a minute in Irish skies to seven to eight instructions a minute in intensely busy UK skies. He would also have to fly with instruments only, meaning he could not rely on looking out the window to get a sense of where he was through visual landmarks, but instead had to use dials and indicators to guide him to a specific destination.

To further complicate his challenge, Gerry would be flying in areas where there was a military presence, which meant he would have to follow further instructions to constantly change height. This was a far cry from what he was used to in Ireland, where he was almost alone in the skies. Gerry sensibly came to me to do some work on his mindset before travelling to the UK, as even thinking about what lay ahead was making him feel overwhelmed. Using the 'Get your head straight' exercise for dealing with overwhelm, we were able to create a system to organise and compartmentalise the subjects of Gerry's overwhelm so that he could approach and execute his exams with ease.

Procrastination

Procrastination can be a complex subject, but I'm going to give you some ideas on how you might approach it and start to unravel it. When we procrastinate, we put off the things we know we need to do and intend to do but don't, because it's hard to find the motivation or we shrink from them out of fear. Procrastination usually prompts feelings of guilt and shame. What is often confusing is that even though you want to achieve or do whatever you are procrastinating about, for some reason you remain stuck, trying to convince yourself that you'll start tomorrow.

Here is an idea to help you manage it. When we are in a state of procrastination and feeling stressed about it, what we tend to focus on is the process of achieving the goal or task. When we are focused on the process, we are looking at what needs to be done: the steps and the actions. We are running a movie in our heads of all the difficult or mundane things that have to happen to reach the outcome. If you are not inspired by that process, you can quickly fall into procrastination. On the other hand, focusing on the end goal can kick-start you into action if your 'why' is inspiring enough.

> **EXERCISE: Find your 'why' and shift your focus**
>
> When you are procrastinating, ask yourself the following:
>
> - Is my 'why' (the reason I want this goal) big enough?
> - Does the outcome inspire me?
> - Am I valuing comfort more than the achievement of this outcome?
>
> If the answer to the last question is yes, ask yourself if you want to keep it that way. In this case, don't beat yourself up – stop chasing the vision, the goal or the outcome, because you just don't want it badly enough.
>
> Next, it's time to do a 'quick flip'.
>
> - First, change your focus around your goal: instead of the process, focus on the outcome. This works a treat if your 'why' is big enough and your outcome sufficiently inspiring.
> - Once you feel inspired by your 'why', return your attention to the process of achieving it and break it into time blocks, task blocks or mini-goals. This allows your mind to organise what needs to happen – it can cope better with smaller, bite-size pieces.
> - Hold on to the inspired feeling and move forward with the action.

DAY THREE: ORDER OUT OF CHAOS

I have found the above exercise to be especially helpful for clients who have a long-term fitness or health goal, as the below client story illustrates.

CASE STUDY: Tina's story

A past client of mine, Tina, had a fitness and weight-loss vision for herself. She came to me to work on her mindset. In the beginning, she was extremely disciplined and all was going well, but as winter arrived she began to find it increasingly difficult to get up in the morning and make it to the gym.

When I questioned her about this, she described what was happening in minute detail. She spoke about how, when the alarm went off, she felt sleepy and cosy in her warm bed. Then she would remember that she had to get up and go to the gym. She would lie in bed and think about getting out from under the warm duvet and the cold air that would greet her. She would then think about getting ready to leave the house, getting into her car and driving to the gym in the cold, dark and silent morning. She would then see herself running on the treadmill, the monitor on the treadmill slowly clocking up the seconds as she waded through the hour.

What was Tina doing? She was running a negative movie in her head before she had even got out of bed. She was consumed by the process of going to the gym and hadn't given a second thought to the outcome: her vision, her dream and her why. I made this clear to Tina and, upon doing so, noted the immediate change in her physiology. She sat up in her chair and her speed of movement increased. She was talking louder and faster, with a lightness in her voice. Her face looked brighter and I could see she was back in motivation mode.

Tina had to take responsibility for achieving her goal. She had to decide to programme herself to focus on her goal when she awoke every morning so that she could avoid any thoughts of the process. After the session, Tina left with some exercises to complete, including recognising the negative movie she was running in her head and creating a new, empowering, movie to replace it with each morning. We decided on a journaling exercise that Tina would complete over the next two weeks: she had to write down fifty things that would happen when she reached her goal, as well as fifty things that would happen if she didn't. This helped Tina to connect with a new compelling outcome, vision and dream – why she wanted to achieve her goal – which distracted her from the process of achieving it. All of this supported her positive progress towards her goal.

Golden Rule 2: Everyone has their own unique model of the world

This Golden Rule is highly effective in supporting people to gain peace and freedom in life. It is based on the idea that if we accept the fact that everyone has their own unique representation or model of how they see the world, we become calmer and less stressed, and can even feel deeper compassion.

To break it down a little more, two people can witness the same situation but have completely different interpretations of what actually happened. These interpretations will be based not only on what they experienced but also on the beliefs and values they

DAY THREE: ORDER OUT OF CHAOS

have acquired through their conditioning and past experiences, both good and bad.

Many of you will be able to recall an event that happened in the past where friends or siblings were also present, and you cannot agree on what actually took place. It's not that anyone is right or wrong; it is just that you have a different perception of what happened and, more importantly, what it meant.

We are often inclined to think that everyone sees the world the way we do, and we can get frustrated when we feel others are not supporting us in some way or another or that they don't get our point of view. However, no one can see the world exactly as we do because we all have had individual experiences that have shaped our perception of the world.

Living by this Golden Rule helps us to understand why people sometimes display seemingly negative and destructive behaviour.

I am not asking you to take on someone's model of their world as your own or condone the behaviour of others. I am merely asking you to see it for what it is. You do not have to like or agree with any specific behaviour, just accept that the other person has a different model of the world and is living in accordance with it.

When you make a big effort to embrace this Golden Rule in your life, you will be able to look at your world and the worlds of others from a completely different perspective. This new perspective gives you a new, detached and often exciting, view of your world. This is where you will start to find your freedom.

Summary

Even though life can feel chaotic at times, there are many ways we can restore order:

- Worry is a process; understanding that and asking ourselves some helpful questions related to the process can ease stress and the fear response.
- Overwhelm is caused by a collection of worrying and stressful thoughts that are all mixed up, creating confusion; the feeling of overwhelm slows and can halt productivity. Use the 'Get your head straight' exercise to take your power back.
- Procrastination stops us from achieving our goals and taking action. Understanding the importance of 'why' you want to do something and achieve the result is key to feeling inspired enough to take action.
- Taking our focus away from the process or mundane actions and towards the inspired 'why' is the way to reach a positive result.
- Acknowledging the fact that we all see the world differently helps us to understand others and their behaviour in a more compassionate and stress-free way.

FIVE
Day Four: Why We Do What We Do

Placing the next piece in the puzzle of ourselves requires a little recap. When I was introducing you to your subconscious mind and using the analogy of the computer, I told you that the hard drive represents the subconscious mind. I also explained that, at birth, the hard drive is empty of memories and experiences and, because of this (among other factors), we have not yet developed any beliefs or values. I also detailed how, in my experience, I have observed that the hard drive is programmed with a default 'happiness programme'. I call this programme the Seven Behavioural Codes®.

Having these seven codes in a balanced state can help us to stay safe and achieve happiness, as well as to thrive and flourish. Sounds simple? It would be if we could just do that, but we tend to complicate things – largely because we are not aware of how we operate.

You may not be aware of it (yet), but you have been striving to fulfil your Seven Behavioural Codes every moment of every day and will continue to do so for the rest of your life. Getting familiar with the Seven Behavioural Codes® will help you to understand your behaviours so that you can change them if desired.

The Seven Behavioural Codes

The Seven Behavioural Codes suggest that we are programmed to seek out the following seven things at every moment of every day:

1. Sureness: survival, safety

2. Diversity: creativity, selection, risk

3. Importance: significance, relevance, identity, raised self-esteem

4. Love: self-love, giving love, receiving love

5. Authentic voice: speaking your truth, being authentic

6. Evolution: growth, progression

7. Connection: no separation, belonging, connection to the source

DAY FOUR: WHY WE DO WHAT WE DO

Balancing these is not necessarily difficult when life is going well. However, as life throws us curve balls, we experience fearful and significant emotional events. When these occur, we can 'traumatise' or imbalance one, two or many of our codes. Our subconscious mind then needs to get these back into balance, doing its best to bring us back to a happy state. Unfortunately, this can result in destructive behaviour – as we will see.

I developed the concept of the seven codes from observing thousands of clients for well over two decades.

Through this observation, I noticed that when people were explaining their stories and the effect those stories were having on their lives, they repeatedly made reference to seven things. The stories were varied and complicated but what was driving the unhappiness, distress, overwhelm, fear and anxiety could be narrowed down to behavioural patterns driven by one, a few or all of these Seven Behavioural Codes.

I have also noticed that, when clients become aware of what they are doing and of the codes that are driving their behaviours, many of them can change these behaviours in an instant. It may not be that easy for everyone, but getting an understanding of the codes underlying your behaviour is the first step on the road to positive change.

Codes, not needs

Just a note: if you are familiar with Abraham Maslow's Hierarchy of Needs, some of the codes may sound similar to some of Maslow's needs.[23] But the Seven Behavioural Codes are not needs. There is an important distinction between codes and needs.

In life, something only becomes a *need* if you are afraid that you are not going to get it. If you *need* to feel safe so that you can feel calm and relaxed, this means that you are afraid of not being or feeling safe.

One of the codes is related to feeling safe but it is not based on a *need*. Taking the example above, when you remove the *need* for safety or the *fear* of not feeling safe, you can just concentrate on feeling safe. Feeling safe then becomes much easier because fear isn't standing in your way. In such a state, where you are fulfilling your code without fear or need, you are one step closer to happiness.

We never mean to hurt

Lastly, before we uncover the codes, it is important to highlight that, as humans, I believe we are not born intending to hurt others or to do damage. Unfortunately, through life experiences, significant emotional events and negative situations, we do get hurt and damaged. In reaction, we set up habits, neural pathways and behavioural patterns to protect ourselves. All the while, we are striving to fulfil our Seven Behavioural Codes.

As a result, all of us at some point will use destructive behaviour to seek the fulfilment of our codes. This can be as extreme and violent as killing someone, or as mild as having a rant about something our mother said to us.

Code 1: Sureness

The first code, sureness, is about survival and safety. We all want to feel safe and secure and to have a sense of certainty. This allows us to feel relaxed and happy. If we have felt unsafe, threatened, violated or insecure at times in our past – which we all have – our subconscious mind will create neural pathways for these uncomfortable feelings.[24]

If there are regular or repeated occasions when we feel unsafe, our urge to feel safe will be heightened because we will subconsciously believe that the world is not safe, which will embed the behavioural pattern more deeply. Therefore, upon experiencing feelings of fear and panic, our subconscious mind will look for ways to make us feel safe and secure, even if the resulting behaviour is negative.

Examples of potentially problematic behaviour related to the first code are being overly cautious or protective and not trusting other people or situations. Violent behaviour can indicate that someone's first code is out of balance, where they feel they need to lash out to keep themselves safe.

TELL-TALE SIGN

If you are running a negative behavioural pattern related to your first code, you may feel emotional discomfort in the pit of your stomach.

Code 2: Diversity

The second code is about creativity, selection and risk. We all love a bit of variety. When we are aligned with this code, we feel alive. If you felt secure and safe as a child, this code will be much easier to align yourself with than if you felt unsafe or under threat regularly, as fear may hold you back from seeking out these experiences.

Empowering behaviours related to this code include trying new hobbies, going on exciting holidays, changing jobs, starting a new career or moving house. For some people, these activities are terrifying. What we feel in relation to this code will be a result of what we have felt in the past about change, risk and diversity.

Have you noticed that this code, related to risk, is almost the opposite of the first code, which is all about safety? Can you imagine a life that revolves completely around safety, or indeed a life that revolves

DAY FOUR: WHY WE DO WHAT WE DO

completely around risk? It would get either boring or exhausting, and neither could provide a consistent feeling of satisfaction. Aligning yourself in a way that keeps all of your codes in balance gives you a better chance of feeling consistently happy.

If there was a lot of fear or threat in your past, your subconscious mind will work hard to override the fear it generated and do its best to make you feel safe (first code). However, 'playing safe' may not allow you to move to this second code, as the risk or diversity experienced through this code would be far too frightening.

I have noticed this with clients who had childhoods during which they felt threatened and unsafe. Their young subconscious minds worked hard at what they thought was keeping them safe, resulting in behaviours driven by fear, overwhelm and stress, and the feeling of being held back. If we allow our lives to be driven by our first code and don't let in some diversity and variety, we end up with a stagnant life lacking in energy.

One problematic behaviour that could be adopted related to our second code is gambling, as it can fulfil a need for risk and excitement. Another example, which might be surprising for some, is overeating – tasting different foods creates excitement if life is dull and uneventful. The same is true of smoking, nail-biting and even drinking alcohol, which can all be used to fulfil this code negatively. You will know that the second code is being fulfilled negatively if the behaviour is having an adverse impact on your life.

Positive behaviours that could fulfil this code include seeking out a new career, learning a new skill, travelling, building a business or looking for a new intimate partner. These examples stay in the positive realm as long as they support you.

TELL-TALE SIGN

If you are running a negative pattern around your second code, you may feel emotional discomfort in the mid-tummy or lower back area.

Code 3: Importance

The third code is about identity, significance, self-esteem and relevance. I could write about this code forever, as it was the one that kept me feeling anxious, depressed and generally in a black tunnel for many years. A sense of significance, feeling relevant and having healthy self-esteem are vital to us all if we want to be happy.

I love to meet people who feel significant and important but without arrogance or ego. Having these feelings is a comfortable, self-assured experience and it demonstrates a strong sense of self-worth. Note that I said, 'I love to meet people who *feel* significant and important.' I did not say, 'I love to meet people who *need* to feel important.'

Remember, when you *need* something it means you are afraid of not having it. If you *need* to feel important that means you are afraid of not feeling important. Fear will then likely play out in your behaviour, showing up as arrogance or aggression, as you will be desperate to feel relevant or important. This can play out in many ways.

People pleasing

On a personal level, because of my past academic failures and the extremely negative feelings I associated with those shortcomings, my third code was well and truly shot. My feelings in that realm were shame, guilt, fear of failure and fear of not being enough, and I had low self-esteem when it came to exams.

As a child, I had always enjoyed the pride and the feeling of being accepted by my father when I had worked hard and achieved good results, and he had acknowledged this. Because I knew how good that felt, I set up a pattern of striving to please and be acknowledged so that I could recreate those feelings of pride, acceptance, relevance, high self-esteem and importance. My subconscious mind ran this pattern automatically to seek out these lovely feelings and make me happy.

Although I felt the negative feelings at a deep level when I failed academically in my teens and again in my early twenties, I pretended everything was fine and I got on with life. However, within the moments of those failures, I created negative feelings that embedded a deep and fear-based new neural pathway. For some time, this pattern was running in the background without any major negative influence; I was only slightly aware of it. The real impact was not revealed until many years later when I had stressed myself through the creation of my natural skincare business.

The business was going great while I was designing and creating the products. However, when it came to selling them, the fear of rejection, failure and not being enough all cascaded from the pattern I had set up many years previously. This escalated to excessive feelings of anxiety that I could not control. As the reality that I wasn't in control unfolded and I wasn't able to get any relief, I fell into intense feelings of hopelessness. I started to feel extremely low, flat and depressed and found it difficult to function at any level.

One way to have stopped these feelings would have been to give up the business. However, because I had created beliefs about myself that I wasn't a quitter and that I had to be strong and resilient, I couldn't bring myself to give up. (There were a lot of other factors involved, but to demonstrate the third code in action, these are the relevant ones.)

DAY FOUR: WHY WE DO WHAT WE DO

People who have had a negative third code-related experience can respond very differently. One example is bullying. I have worked with many bullies and part of their pattern is related to the third code. When someone *needs* to bully, it is often because they are afraid of looking or feeling irrelevant or unimportant, and their self-esteem is low.

Think about it for a minute. One of the quickest ways of going from feeling irrelevant to feeling important is to make someone *else* feel irrelevant. If I make you feel irrelevant by bullying you, my subconscious mind believes it is fulfilling my third code, even though my behaviour is destructive. When you understand *why* someone is doing something, it is easier not to be judgemental. This doesn't mean we condone that behaviour, but by not being judgemental we keep ourselves regulated.

Other examples of negative behaviours that the subconscious mind may believe support the third code include violence towards another, throwing tantrums, seeking attention through destructive behaviours, being dishonest, being obsessed with gaining material wealth, or even participating in dangerous sports or activities. It is the intention behind the behaviour that determines whether it is destructive or not. To assess a behavioural pattern related to your third code, ask yourself if the intention is driven by a *need* to feel important or relevant. If the answer is yes, then the pattern may be destructive.

TELL-TALE SIGN

If you are running a negative pattern around your third code, you may feel emotional discomfort in your solar plexus – the area at the top of your tummy, just below the breastbone.

Code 4: Love

It is within the fourth code, which is about self-love, giving and receiving love, that I have observed we have the most difficulty. Without generalising too much, many of us are conditioned to put others first and not be seen to be too kind to ourselves.

It is easy to see how it can make you feel happy when you show love, give love, receive love and practise self-love.

Positive behaviours that fulfil this code include helping others, caring for someone, doing good without needing recognition and just being kind. Feeling comfortable with receiving kindness is also a positive behaviour related to this code.

For our subconscious mind to fulfil this code, we often also play out destructive behaviours like overeating, smoking or nail-biting, which are all quick ways to comfort ourselves (a distorted kind of self-love). This pattern is established, for example, when someone first tries a nice food and notices the feeling of comfort

DAY FOUR: WHY WE DO WHAT WE DO

they get. Roll the movie forward to a day when you don't feel so good and your subconscious mind reminds you of a quick way to feel better. The next step is to go and find nice food to eat (even though your hunger is more emotional than physical) and have a good old nosh. In some cases, though, this is quickly followed by feelings of guilt.

Remember what we learned about the subconscious mind: even though it runs 95% of the processing capability of your mind, it is only programmed to make you feel happy. Eating tasty food is an easy way to achieve that happiness for some, but the subconscious mind is only focused on the present moment and not on the future consequences. Once you have had the nice food and felt good for a few minutes the guilt often kicks in, making you feel miserable. Ringing any bells?

Going back to the example of bullying related to the third code, you can see how bullying behaviour can also fulfil this fourth code. When a bully engages in that behaviour and feels relevant as a result, this can also give them a sense of comfort and be a destructive means of self-love.

You want to regularly experience this fourth code being fulfilled by positive behaviour. Allowing yourself to receive love from somebody close to you, or even from a pet, is a great way to align with this code. If you find this difficult, please be gentle with yourself. A struggle here indicates hurt in the past, so letting love in may be challenging. It relates to a fear of being hurt, and we often create resistance to dropping a fear if we have experienced something particularly traumatic.

TELL-TALE SIGN

If you are running a negative pattern around your fourth code, you may feel emotional discomfort in your heart and chest.

Code 5: Authentic voice

It is important for us all to feel we can speak our truth without inviting a backlash. There are many ways of being authentic and speaking your truth. The first, and the most obvious, is to say the words. Sometimes, though, it is best not to speak your truth face-to-face (you might end up lonely and friendless), but you can get it out by writing a tell-all letter that you don't need to send.

Other ways of expressing your authentic self are through the clothes you wear, the hobbies you enjoy, the books you read and the friends you keep. All of these things represent a part of your truth and what is important to you.

If you feel stifled or frustrated, this could be a sign of your subconscious mind telling you that you're selling yourself short. Look at all the areas of your life and see if you are regularly being true to yourself.

If you have experienced ridicule when you tried to speak up or express yourself in the past, your subconscious mind will not want you to feel that discomfort again. One way the subconscious could deal with this feeling is to run a pattern of pretence to deflect from the truth. This is the work of the ego, creating a social mask to hide the truth of the real you, which the ego is afraid to reveal in case people don't like the authentic you and you get hurt.

You will likely see many people around you who display patterns of pretence. This could manifest in pretending to be smarter, happier, richer and more intelligent than they really are. This is just their ego's fear of showing the real them.

TELL-TALE SIGN
If you are running a negative pattern around your fifth code, you may feel emotional discomfort in your throat.

Code 6: Evolution

This code is about growth and progression. If we are not growing, we are stagnant or dying. Fulfilling this sixth code brings so much energy, joy, growth, expansion and vitality. Our conditioning plays a big role in blocking this code: in the past, when you stepped outside your comfort zone to progress and grow, the experience might have been too overwhelming.

Progressing and growing give you purpose and meaning, and a reason to get up in the morning. They get you excited about life. There are many ways in which we can progress and grow, including through education, spirituality, personal growth, careers, businesses, health, finances, relationships and even hobbies.

This sixth code is closely related to the second code of creativity, diversity, selection and risk. Imbalance in our third code (self-esteem, relevance, importance and identity) or our first code (feeling safe) can also get in the way of us aligning with this code.

TELL-TALE SIGN

If you are running a negative pattern around this code – that is, if you have a strong desire to progress and grow but are being held back by fear from past experiences in the earlier codes – you may feel emotions of frustration and yearning.

Code 7: Connection

There is great comfort in feeling that you belong and are connected to something or someone. This seventh code ranges from the most fundamental forms of connection and lack of separation to an expanded consciousness.

The first, most fundamental form of connection is where you have a sense of belonging within yourself. This comes with practising self-love and being comfortable with who you are. The next fundamental form is in a partnership of two people, whether that's an intimate relationship, friendship, business relationship or one with siblings. It's a feeling of not being alone. The progression from the fundamental connection is belonging to a group, which could be your class in school/college or a sports team. This progresses up through the levels of county, country, continent, world and universe.

When we connect at the universal level, we feel a deep sense of belonging to the source. This idea that there is no separateness helps us to attain spiritual growth and progression, and ultimately a sense of peace. When there is no separateness there can be no competition or comparison. There is only collaboration, community and contribution.

If you are not fulfilling this code on some level, you are most likely not fulfilling many of the other codes either, as it is difficult to feel safe, significant and loved when we are not connected to something or someone outside ourselves. This may be due to conditioning or past experiences, in which you learned that it is not safe to connect. A great way to work on fulfilling this code is to start contributing without expecting any recognition in return, such as random acts of kindness or charity work where you give just because you can.

TELL-TALE SIGN

If you are not fulfilling the seventh code at any level, you will feel a sense of disconnection.

The good news is, when you fulfil this code at a high level you feel it physically and energetically in every cell of your body. Beware, the sensation is addictive!

Now that you know the seven codes, you can think about how they show up for you and what your behaviour might reveal.

> **EXERCISE: Observe your codes**
>
> Take some time today to observe one behaviour that you engage in but would prefer not to and investigate which code or codes you may be looking to align with through that behaviour. Being aware of why we do something can be the catalyst for change, so it is worth spending some time on this exercise.

Golden Rule 3: There is a positive intention behind all behaviour

When we understand the Seven Behavioural Codes, living by the next Golden Rule becomes easier. This Golden Rule requires that we assume that a person engaging in a behaviour is driven by a subconscious positive intention.

We have already established that all behaviour is driven by our subconscious minds in a bid to fulfil our Seven Behavioural Codes and, as this is done to protect us and make us happy, it has a positive intention. Behaviour, though, can at times be destructive or even violent, where past fearful experiences have resulted in imbalances in our codes. The negative behaviour is a subconscious bid to bring us back to balance; even though it can be destructive, the intention of the subconscious mind is always positive (for the person engaging in the behaviour).

Living by this Golden Rule makes it so much easier not to get caught up in the drama, the story and the negativity. You will notice that you are seeing the world from an elevated view. This new perspective enables you to look down and understand why something is the way it is, without judgement.

Summary

Although we may not be aware of it, the way we behave from one minute to the next is governed by behavioural codes that we have been evolving since childhood:

- The Seven Behavioural Codes describe potential subconscious programmes that drive our behaviours and influence our happiness. Understanding these codes is important, as they impact our behaviours.

- Aligning with these codes – feeling safe, embracing diversity, recognising our importance, experiencing love, expressing our authentic voice, seeking growth and feeling connected – leads to happiness and wellbeing.

- Negative experiences and fears can disrupt the balance of these codes, leading to destructive behaviours.

- By embracing the Golden Rule of choosing to see a positive intention behind all behaviour, we can self-regulate more easily and stay detached from stress and drama.

SIX
Day Five: Influences Of Our Past

The Britannica Dictionary definition of memory is 'the encoding, storage, and retrieval in the human mind of past experiences'.[25] Our experiences in life become memories or collections of information from the past. Once we have experienced an event, it becomes a snapshot in time.

Memories and beliefs

To make sense of memories, we need to give them meaning. This is based on our interpretation of what we experienced at the time of the event as well as previous memories from our past. This shapes what we believe to be true about a situation, and about everything and everyone involved in it – hence, it is the birth of a belief. In tandem, we also subconsciously create an emotional response to the memory, which helps us decide on our behaviour or the action we take next in relation to that memory and our new belief.

Even though we may have many good memories, the subconscious mind will tend to focus on the bad ones, because of our default negative bias. It often puts these memories on a continuous loop of thoughts to help the conscious mind make sense of them or find a solution. When this happens, we can feel like we are trapped in a cycle of overwhelm, stress or worry.

To help us get relief and manage the pain of this loop, applying the 'Problem not problem' technique from Day Two and considering the stages of worry described in Day Three will be helpful. Both will help reduce the negative feelings associated with stressful memories.

When our subconscious mind creates and embeds a belief, even if it is a small and relatively insignificant belief like 'I am punctual', it is wired by default to search for references and memories to support that belief. Because it deems this belief to be true, it can dismiss any information that might challenge it.

As your subconscious mind embeds the belief it has created as a truth, it will continually refer to it when deciding what behaviour to carry out. If you believe 'I am punctual' you will automatically carry out behaviours to support that belief, unless you consciously decide not to.

The behaviours related to this belief can cause stress or relief, depending on how well informed you are in this area of personal development. You will understand by now that no belief is right or wrong, good or bad. It is just a belief. To identify whether something is an empowering belief just ask yourself, 'Does this belief serve me?'

CASE STUDY: Patricia's story

I worked with a client called Patricia who came to me because she was late for every appointment and wanted to change. After some questioning, we discovered that for three months, when she was ten, her father had to collect her daily and repeatedly told her that she was always late. As a result, she subconsciously created the belief about herself that she was 'always late'. This subconscious belief continued to drive her behaviour, making sure this remained true for her, resulting in her indeed being late. When we looked at her life more closely, of course there were many occasions when she was on time, but her subconscious was focusing on the times she was late, as this is what it believed to be true about her.

To help her overcome this problem, we reversed the belief that was embedded in her subconscious mind to a more positive belief: 'I am punctual.' Beliefs are not just statements; they also have feelings attached to them. Patricia's belief of 'I am always late' had feelings of hopelessness and shame attached to it, which she experienced as physical sensations in her body, and they were driving her behaviour. By changing her belief to 'I am punctual', Patricia began to feel more hopeful that this behaviour could change. Then we released the feelings of shame and hopelessness from her body, using a belief change process, and replaced them with new feelings of confidence. This helped Patricia to change her behaviour and had a significant positive impact on her punctuality.

Limited control

Our beliefs are so important because, coupled with our values, they are the main drivers of our behaviours, which directly lead to our results in life. If you want to change something about your life, start by understanding your beliefs and values and identifying which ones serve you in terms of what you want to achieve. If you change the appropriate ones, your behaviour changes and so do your results.

With this in mind, remember that the subconscious mind is incredibly powerful and instigates so much automatic behaviour based on its beliefs. This explains why the logic and willpower of the conscious mind can only control behaviour in the short term. To take control of the subconscious mind, we would need to constantly remind ourselves to engage the conscious mind to override the automatic subconscious patterns that are running in the background. This would be exhausting and not particularly successful. A much more efficient way to change behaviour is to change the underlying beliefs and patterns and to release the emotions attached to memories. This gives us the freedom to move forward in a powerful and positive way.

DAY FIVE: INFLUENCES OF OUR PAST

As well as disempowering, limiting beliefs, we can create empowering, expansive beliefs. You have already created thousands of beliefs that are influencing your behaviour every moment of every day, though you may not be aware of them. Examples of some disempowering beliefs are:

- I am lazy.
- I don't have any confidence.
- I am not smart.
- Everyone else is better than me.

Some examples of negative beliefs that I have seen especially among businesswomen and some students that I have worked with are:

- I don't know enough.
- I am not good enough.
- I am not successful.
- I am not a businesswoman.
- It has to be perfect.

Examples of empowering beliefs are:

- I am confident and competent.
- I have the resources to be successful.
- I am focused.
- I am caring.

99

Again, the more of these statements you truly believe and feel, the easier it will be for you to thrive and flourish.

I cannot put into words how wonderful it is to see a client flip a negative belief that has been holding them back for years into a positive, empowering belief, and then witness the change in their behaviour and results.

Moving to a conviction

If our beliefs are connected to a strong enough emotional charge, we will search for more and more references to validate that they are true until we embed them as a deep conviction. Convictions are highly energetic and infused with passion. They have the power to move nations to glory; they also have the power to destroy nations. If beliefs can do that to a nation, what can they do for you?

Again, like beliefs, a conviction is neither right nor wrong, neither good nor bad. It is just a conviction. The question to ask yourself is, 'Is my conviction good for me, for my family and my wider community?' If the answer is yes, then it is a good conviction for you. When working on changing a conviction, the process is the same as changing a belief.

Our beliefs can be broken into three main categories:

- Beliefs about ourselves
- Beliefs about others

DAY FIVE: INFLUENCES OF OUR PAST

- Beliefs about our environment – our physical, social and political surroundings

To get started on changing some of your limiting beliefs, the following two-part exercise focuses on beliefs about ourselves. Starting here will have a profound impact on your personal positive change.

> **EXERCISE: Deciphering beliefs**
>
> For the first part of this exercise, take some time out to reflect on your thoughts, emotions and behaviours, paying particular attention to recurring patterns or negative self-talk that may indicate underlying limiting beliefs.
>
> - Ask yourself, 'What beliefs do I hold about myself that may be holding me back?' These beliefs usually start with 'I am...' or 'I am not...'
> - Look back at significant events or moments in your life where you felt stuck, where you failed or where you avoided certain opportunities.
> - Ask yourself, 'What beliefs or thoughts about myself were present during those times?'
>
> Once you have written down some disempowering beliefs about yourself, ask yourself the following questions:
>
> - What evidence do you have to support your limiting belief about yourself?
> - Have you ever achieved or experienced something that contradicts your current belief?

> If so, what was it and how did you manage to do it? (Dig deep on this one.)
> - What would you do differently if you didn't hold this limiting belief about yourself?
> - Can you think of someone who has faced similar challenges and overcome them? What can you learn from their experience?
> - How would your life be different if you let go of this limiting belief and started believing in your abilities?
> - What steps can you take right now to challenge this belief and prove it wrong?
> - What would you say to a close friend who held the same belief about themselves? How would you encourage and support them in changing it?
> - If you had unlimited resources and support, what would you attempt to achieve? How does that challenge your current belief about yourself?

Values: What is important?

Your values are the things that are important to you and that you prioritise in life. You develop your values in a similar way to your beliefs. You first observe your reality, then assign it meaning and decide what is important to you.

From the moment you are born, many things influence this process. The 'Imprint period' is the time in your life that influences your values most. The imprint period, according to Morris Massey, is the first five to seven years of life; during this period, we soak up every bit of information we receive.[26]

Because we have not consciously developed the ability to be objective and discerning during this time, we are greatly influenced by what we observe and develop beliefs and values in relation to everything we experience. The people and things that influence us most at this stage of life include our carers, culture, religion, geography and climate, to mention a few. These influences ultimately impact the core values we create for our lives.

Your guiding compass

Your beliefs and values are your compass; they guide and direct you through life. Although it's important to have goals, it is your beliefs and values that will determine whether you reach them. Examples of values are honesty, love, integrity, truth, companionship, safety, success, family, health, wealth and passion.

Let me reiterate: what you believe to be true and what you value in life form the compass that navigates your journey through life, and they are the biggest determinant of your results.

At this point, we have an exercise to help you identify some of your values. It is important to be honest with yourself when listing what you currently value concerning your goals in life. For example, if your goal is to meet an intimate partner and you are saying that your values in relation to this goal are love, companionship, fun and humour, but you are sitting at home not making an effort to go out and meet people, then I can tell you now that you value safety and comfort more than you value a relationship.

It's simple. If you want to make things happen, realise that you will be influenced by your strongest values in relation to those things. If your top values are comfort and safety, you will always strive to be comfortable and safe, which could translate into a mediocre life. This is fine if this is what you want, but if you have goals that don't tally with this, you may need to rethink your values.

> **EXERCISE: Identifying your values**
>
> Below are some questions that can serve as a starting point for exploring your values. Ask yourself:
>
> - What brings you a deep sense of fulfilment and joy? Think about experiences, activities or moments in your life where you have felt truly alive and fulfilled. What values or principles were being honoured during those times? For example, if travelling and exploring new cultures brought you joy, it might indicate that you value adventure, curiosity and open-mindedness.
> - What aspects of your life are non-negotiable? Consider the areas that you prioritise and are unwilling to compromise on. This could be

your relationships, career, personal growth, health or any other domain. Reflect on why they are so important to you and what values they represent. For instance, if you prioritise your health and wellbeing, it might indicate that you value self-care, vitality or balance.

- What qualities and characteristics do you admire in others? Think about people you look up to, either in your personal life or in the public domain. Identify the specific qualities, traits or actions that you find inspiring and admirable. This again can give you insights into your values. For example, if you admire honesty, integrity and authenticity in others, it suggests that those values are significant to you as well.

Remember that values are unique to everyone, and they may evolve over time. Taking the time to reflect on and connect with your values can provide guidance and clarity in making decisions, setting goals and living a more authentic and fulfilling life.

What is the meaning of it all?

Earlier, we briefly discussed meaning, but it is important enough to warrant a section all to itself. From the day we are born, we are living through experiences, and processing the information we observe through our five senses of sight, hearing, smell, taste and touch.

After we have put information through these processes, we then subconsciously create an opinion around whether it's true, whether we like it, whether it will help us in some way, whether it will make us feel comfortable and whether others will approve. In doing this, we are investing our experiences with meaning. This meaning helps to build our unique model or representation of the world. This is neither right nor wrong, it is just *our* meaning, and it is essential to our existence because it helps us to function.

Remember that meaning is created by subconscious decisions; we are rarely conscious of meaning when we are creating it.

Parent panic stations

I often see concerned parents who feel guilty about some of the things they have said to their children, or when they think of negative behaviours they may have displayed in front of their children. They worry that they have scarred them for life.

If this rings a bell with you, please let your fears be allayed. I am of course not encouraging you to say anything negative to your children, but know that you have no control over the meaning your child decides to put on what they observe. In fact, a small child will most likely not even be consciously aware of the meaning they are giving to what they are observing.

The most important thing in supporting your child and helping them to create a healthy representation of their world is to make sure they feel loved. This needs to be done through your actions as well as your words.

Golden Rule 4: Practise non-judgement of others

With a deeper understanding that we all behave according to our beliefs and values, and try to fulfil our Seven Behavioural Codes, and when living by our previous Golden Rule of respecting that everyone has their own unique model of the world, it becomes much easier to practise non-judgement.

To understand this Golden Rule, you need to know the distinction between judging and judgement. When we make a judgement (rather than being judgemental), we are weighing up the pros and cons of a situation and deciding on what to do or where to go next with the issue.

We all need to make judgements, as it helps us to compare and contrast things in life so that we can make decisions – decisions about everything from the food we buy to the school we send our children to, the job we aspire to have and the person we want to spend the rest of our lives with. If we didn't assess the different options and their possible consequences, we would never make a decision.

By contrast, the word 'judgemental', according to the Oxford Dictionary definition, means 'inclined to make moral judgements; having or displaying an overly critical point of view'.[27] The fourth Golden Rule requires you to practise being non-judgemental towards others, by not being critical or pass-remarkable and, more importantly, not sharing your criticisms with others.

You already understand why people do what they do: it is always related to fulfilling their Seven Behavioural Codes, which may have been distorted because of fear. These don't necessarily need to be big fears like acts of violence or major accidents. Fear is relevant, no matter what the scale: even the negative processing of a casual comment from a teacher can be insidious, embedding a disempowering pattern.

We are all judgemental to a degree because we are human, and it can be difficult to stop ourselves. Typically, judging others is propelled by our need to feel safe, relevant, important and loved (the first, third and fourth codes). If we have an imbalance around these codes, we will be subconsciously tempted to judge others. This is because in comparing ourselves with others in an attempt to prove we are better or right, we fulfil the needs of our ego and ease our subconscious mind's fear of not feeling safe, sure, relevant, important and loved. If you are committed to your positive change, you will embrace this rule and drop the need to judge others so that you can stop feeling those fears.

If you feel you are abiding by this Golden Rule and living a life of non-judgement, I am not here to judge (excuse the pun) and say otherwise. However, I do challenge you to take it to the next level.

Who do we judge most?

The people we tend to be most judgemental about are those closest to us, so the first target is often ourselves. We will listen to that negative and self-critical voice in our heads. Next on the list are those whom we love most. We judge them because we want them to be their best, or we want them to make us happy because we are not taking responsibility for our happiness. We can also judge them because we have a need to control. Whatever the reason is, don't beat yourself up about it. Just start practising non-judgement in all areas, with all people.

To do this and begin living a less judgemental life, start by looking at who you judge most and be brutally honest with yourself about why. Then, remind yourself that when this person was born, they did not intend to hurt or offend or damage anyone. It is so important to accept this and to understand that their positive and negative conditioning and experiences, along with their need to align themselves with their Seven Behavioural Codes, made them the way they are. Being non-judgemental does not mean accepting or condoning behaviour that does not fit with your values; it just means assessing it objectively rather than criticising the person.

In being non-judgemental, you can still approach someone and explicitly tell them how you feel about their attitude or behaviour. However, you will notice that you are not overly emotionally charged if you have let go of the judgement. Embracing this rule has made my life and the lives of thousands of my clients so much easier and more peaceful. We can voice our opinions calmly and still be heard.

Summary

Although we are not usually aware of it, our behaviour is determined by our beliefs and values, which impacts our results:

- Some beliefs serve us; others don't.
- We can change our beliefs and free ourselves from negative patterns of behaviour.
- Identifying negative patterns of behaviour and self-talk is the first step to replacing them with positive ones.
- Your beliefs and values are the biggest determinants of what you can achieve in life.

DAY FIVE: INFLUENCES OF OUR PAST

- You must be honest with yourself about how your values relate to your goals.
- You have no control over the meaning that others may place on your behaviour.
- Judging is fine, being judgemental is not.
- You can remove the emotional charge from situations by adopting a calm and rational approach in communicating to others your feelings about their behaviour.

SEVEN
Day Six: Making The Most Of Mini Miens

Within us, we all have access to incredible resources to instigate change. Motivation, courage, determination, confidence, balance, perspective and many more. You have as much access to these qualities as everyone else. In this chapter, you will learn how these resources are closely connected to pre-existing aspects of your personality. Becoming familiar with these parts of yourself is vital for positive growth.

Introducing the Mini Miens

In Chapter One we touched on how our personalities have various aspects and how different aspects are in control at different times and in different situations. I refer to these aspects as Mini Miens®. Understanding them can have a profound effect on how we live our lives.

In this chapter, you will learn what your miens are, and how they have been affecting you throughout your life without you being aware of it. The information presented here comes from the body of work I created and teach, called Quantum Thinking Transformation, or QTT®.

The Oxford Dictionary definition of a mien is: 'The look, bearing, manner, or conduct of a person, as showing character and mood.'[28] We all have a variety of Mini Miens, mini aspects of our personality. Some of these miens consist of moods, characteristics and behaviours that disempower us and can be in constant conflict with other miens within us that want us to be aligned, balanced and happy.

I'll describe a range of miens below, but examples include your Motivator and your Victim.

At times we can all feel a bit overwhelmed, or as if our internal conflicts are driving us nuts. These conflicts are caused by the grappling of these different aspects of ourselves. Many clients come to me because they think they are going mad. Part of them wants to be or do one thing, and another part of them wants to be or do the complete opposite. For example, one part of a person might want to be healthy, fit, eat well and exercise regularly, and another part of them just wants to sit on the sofa and eat a bar of chocolate. The two miens in conflict here are most likely their Motivator and their Rebel.

I'm familiar with this particular conflict, having experienced it myself many times. Past conflicts of mine include a battle between the part of me that wanted to keep smoking cigarettes and the part that wanted to give up; between the part of me that wanted to play small in my business and the part that wanted to play big and reach out to as many people as possible.

When I first started learning techniques and tools to deal with these patterns, I used to reconcile these miens with a neurolinguistic programming (NLP) technique called Parts Integration.[29] But as time went on and I gained more experience and better results, I discovered more profound and lasting ways of aligning the different aspects of ourselves.

Identifying the Mini Miens

The miens, or different aspects of you, that I keep referring to are like mini personalities. I'm not suggesting that you are suffering from multiple-personality disorder, but I'm sure you can identify different aspects of your personality.

THE SEVEN-DAY POSITIVITY PROJECT

There is no definitive list of miens, as they are personal to the individual, but there is a short list of examples below for you to ponder. I highly recommend that you create your own list of all your miens. Becoming familiar with them can be a real eye-opener in your pursuit of long-term, positive change. Remember, they are aspects of you, not separate from you.

Here are some examples of Mini Miens can we can likely all identify with:

- **Motivator:** the aspect of you that is motivated, driven and focused, and can move mountains.
- **Preacher:** the aspect of you that tells it like it is, when necessary.
- **Superhero:** the aspect of you that can take and keep control, help others, set a good example and be resourceful.
- **Entertainer:** the aspect of you that is capable of entertaining others. (Even if you haven't exercised this aspect in a while, the capability is within you.)
- **Carer:** the aspect of you that is capable of looking after yourself and others.
- **Victim:** the aspect of you that allows you to feel sorry for yourself. (We all have this.)
- **Project manager:** the aspect of you that is capable of organising what needs to get done.

DAY SIX: MAKING THE MOST OF MINI MIENS

- **Cynic:** the aspect of you that believes people are motivated by self-interest rather than unselfish or honourable reasons.
- **Doubter:** the aspect of you that doubts and questions, and is reluctant to trust.
- **Warrior:** the aspect of you that is capable of showing courage and resilience.

Here is a further list of more specific aspects we may have, but it is by no means complete – what would you add to it for yourself?

- Addict
- Angel
- Risk-taker
- Goddess
- Leader
- Martyr
- Mediator
- Teacher
- Hermit
- Connector/networker
- Rescuer
- Saboteur
- Good Samaritan
- Servant
- Rebel
- Student
- Visionary
- Businessperson
- Sceptic

As children, we dip seamlessly in and out of all of our miens. If you watch a small child playing, you will see how quickly they can jump from one mood to another, one behaviour to another and one mini personality to another. They enjoy the full range of these aspects, and at a young age, it is natural to display them all without inhibition. As we get older, there are many other miens that we think we should no longer play out, like our Fairy, Rock Star or Superhero miens, as we can become conditioned to believe these are silly or inappropriate behaviours for an adult.

But if you think about it, being willing to embrace those 'silly' miens could be beneficial when we need to problem-solve or access courage or confidence. The Superhero and Rock Star often have great ideas and can be brave. Instead, we are conditioned to believe we should remain serious and strong, relying on a more straightlaced aspect, like Captain Sensible.

As we progress through the years, we can get stuck in just a few miens because they are familiar and feel safe, in line with our first behavioural code. However, if we allow ourselves to be limited in this way and accept a small number of miens as our whole identity, it can stunt our growth and development on so many levels and prevent us from seeing how we could change.

When we experience fear, big or small, some of these miens will come to the rescue and help us cope. When frightened, we take on the manner and mood of the Mini Mien we subconsciously believe will best cope with the situation. If we get too reliant on or subconsciously attached to the help of these miens, they can stick around for years after the initial fear has passed and can disempower us as they continue to play out their fears, beliefs and behaviours.

Examples of this would be the Victim or the Doubter Mini Miens. These miens are not bad. No single aspect of a personality is good or bad as such; they all have benefits and drawbacks. It's a matter of deciding which are valuable to you in different situations.

Beware of becoming reliant on your Victim to help you feel comfort in times of fear: it can be highly destructive if you are living it all of the time. We all embody our Victim now and again because it permits us to wallow in self-pity and self-comfort. This can feel good, especially when accompanied by a tub of ice-cream. However, staying with your Victim long term can result in an unhappy and unfulfilled life.

Your doubter can be just as destructive, or even more so. This is clear in the story below, of a young man who embodied his Doubter mien to protect himself and how it threatened his quality of life.

CASE STUDY: David's story

I worked with David, a keen and successful sportsman, in his early thirties. He had gone through some significant emotional events in school at the age of twelve. Because of his experiences with teachers in school and his religious conditioning, he had created a subconscious belief that the world was not safe (first code).

At that time, David's Doubter came to the rescue and, as the young man embodied this Mini Mien, he started questioning almost everything in his life. He did this because the events had made him feel unsafe. By doubting everything, his subconscious mind believed he was keeping himself on guard. His Doubter thought it was doing a great job, but even though the events were over and he was safe, it had set up a neural pathway that continually triggered fear. Although David's life was great on paper, over the years the intensity of his doubt increased so much that, by the time he came to me, he was crippled with fear 70% of the time.

In our first session, we used curiosity questions and behavioural codes to unearth the behavioural pattern he was running. Upon acknowledging the existence of this pattern, David experienced immediate relief as his fear level dropped from a ten to a one.

At the end of the session, we planned for him to just carry on with his life as usual for a week, which often meant putting himself in situations that would trigger his fear. During the first three days, he enjoyed relief like he had never known. No matter what situation he put himself in, the old fear was not triggered. He felt comfortable and revelled in the freedom of being able to go where he wanted and communicate with whomever he chose without feeling any fear.

On the fourth day, David noticed that he had started questioning his relief. This was the work of his Doubter Mini Mien. The more he allowed his Doubter to take over his thoughts and self-talk, the quicker he convinced himself that he could feel some fear coming back. He then fell into a feeling of disappointment and started telling himself, 'I knew it was too good to be true', 'I will never get relief' and 'I told you so'. David returned to me seven days after his first appointment, as planned, and I asked questions to find out exactly what had happened during the week. I listened intently on all levels and could again hear the voice of the Doubter. (The Doubter's speech patterns include lots of 'Yes, but...')

Once we had identified the reappearance of David's Doubter, we looked specifically at what it was trying to achieve and whether it was serving him. David was clear that it was not, and that choosing to embody new Mini Miens in these situations would serve him better. David's choice was to instead embody his Warrior and Motivator Mini Miens, with whom he was familiar from his sporting activities, and to use these to render his Doubter redundant. Years on, he is still enjoying a more open, less fearful life.

Each mien has both positive and negative aspects – light and shadow. Below, I describe what these are for some of the more common miens.

Light and shadow of Victim

When your Victim is playing out in full, it can have a positive impact since it allows you to self-comfort (fourth code – self-love). On the negative side, it causes you to feel miserable and stuck. It does this all at the same time. It can also have a secondary-gain motive, in that it wants you to feel miserable so that others will feel sorry for you, which, in turn, would make you feel loved (fourth code – receiving love).

Light and shadow of Motivator

From a positive perspective, when your Motivator is playing out in full it allows you to feel safe and sure (first code); enjoy variety and risk (second code); feel relevant (third code) and authentic (fifth code); show self-love (fourth code); experience progress and growth (sixth code); and even feel a sense of belonging (seventh code). That is a lot on the positive side, but the Motivator can also have a negative effect when it is driven by fear of failure and pushes you towards burn-out, exhaustion or illness. The codes being fulfilled in the shadow are most likely the motivation to feel safe (first code), the motivation to feel relevant (third code) and the motivation to feel self-love (fourth code).

Light and shadow of Rebel

I have to mention the Rebel Mini Mien as it is one that I see a lot in clients. I love the Rebel, as it stands up for what it believes in and is not afraid to fight for it. However, on the negative side, I have noticed that the Rebel Mini Mien can stop clients from conquering disempowering or destructive behaviours, like smoking or overeating. The Rebel often decides that it will not be told what to do, or that it does not want to conform to the ideas of other aspects of the client, like the Motivator.

DAY SIX: MAKING THE MOST OF MINI MIENS

In this instance, I would get the client to tune into their Rebel to recognise which codes this Mini Mien is trying to fulfil. It is typically safety and sureness (first code), risk (second code) – you can see how trying to reconcile these two contradictory codes might give rise to stress or anxiety – relevance (third code), self-love (fourth code) and authentic voice (fifth code). The client may have felt pushed, forced or pressured into doing things in the past that didn't sit right with them. Their Rebel rightly came to their rescue then, and it is still playing out now, but in a disempowering way. Use your Rebel wisely.

The miens you spend most time embodying are the ones that have dictated your results to date. If you are not happy with your results, you can choose new, more appropriate, miens to step into after you have done some alignment work on the ones that aren't serving you. Once you have created a list of the miens you embody regularly and those you have embodied in the past, you can choose which miens you want to use to create your future.

It's important to recognise that though these miens are not separate from you, neither are they you. They are just aspects of you that you subconsciously embody to get results, and their behaviour, as ever, is driven by the Seven Behavioural Codes. It saddens me to see people who live in two or three low-key or fearful miens because it is all they know when they could be living the aspects of themselves that are full of joy, bliss, happiness, laughter, love and growth. Now that you are aware of what Mini Miens are and what they do, you are empowered with the choice to embrace those that will allow you to enjoy your life.

> **EXERCISE: Mini Miens**
>
> To start exploring your Mini Miens and the effect they are having on your life:
>
> - List the different areas of your life at present – examples would be career/job, health, relationships, finances, hobbies etc.
> - Identify your behaviour in each area, both positive and negative behaviours, to get a true picture.
> - Ask yourself which mien you call on in each situation.
> - Now ask yourself if each of these Mini Miens serves you.
> - If they do, great. If they don't, choose to embody a different mien that will support you in that situation.
>
> When asking yourself these kinds of questions, remember that the evidence always lies in your behaviour. Whether positive or negative, your behaviour is always what creates your results.

Listening to the Mini Miens

Self-talk is something that we do all the time. That little voice is yapping away in our heads every moment of every day. It's a voice that some people may not even be aware that they're hearing. Often, when I point this out to people, it's the first time that they've acknowledged it. Perhaps they say to themselves, 'What voice?' and it's then that they recognise it.

Self-talk has the power to destroy you or to elevate you to your highest level of joy. Remember, it is the voice of a Mini Mien that you are speaking with at any given time. What your self-talk is saying to you and how strongly you agree with it makes all the difference. I am referring here to a single voice, but there can be many.

The voices of these Mini Miens are talking in your head for all of your waking hours and, for the most part, you will listen to them without being aware of it. If they have strong opinions about you or your representation of the world, this will affect how you think, what you believe, how you behave and, ultimately, your results in life.

As we already know, your subconscious mind is a master at carrying out instructions. If your self-talk is coming from your Inner Critic Mini Mien, the results can be catastrophic. If your self-talk is that of a motivated, confident Mini Mien like your Superhero or Motivator, it will be empowering and will serve you well in your pursuit of happiness.

Unfortunately, I've found that a large proportion of the population listens to negative, critical self-talk every day. If this strikes a chord with you, consider embodying a different Mini Mien – one that speaks to you in a supportive way.

Golden Rule 5: You have all the resources you need

When you consider the challenges that people have overcome and the goals they have achieved in the history of the world, it is nothing short of incredible. To overcome and achieve we need a set of resources. Fortunately, we are all born with them. Every one of us has within us everything we need to create positive change. If you haven't yet created the life you want, you may think that you do not have these resources. You do; it's just that you haven't known how to access and deploy them.

I know some of us have been dealt a worse hand in life than others. I also know that life throws curve balls all the time. However, when it does, we can access the resources to deal with them. We can look for solutions and be motivated, proactive, resourceful, positive, driven and focused. We also have the resources to endure pain, trust, accept, learn and everything else we might need to improve any situation. However, when the going gets tough, we often rely on de-motivation, a victim attitude, blame, violence, anger, scepticism, cynicism, apathy and many other negative traits that will disempower us and make life miserable. Why do we do this? Remember: it is not our fault. It is the result of our programming.

You will have already tapped into your resources many times over the years. Use the exercise below to discover what they are.

> **EXERCISE: Finding your resources**
>
> The following exercise will help you to identify the resources you have within you, and move towards your goals:
>
> 1. List 100 things that you have achieved over the years. They can be big or small achievements; I recommend that you list both.
> 2. Take each achievement and list all the resources that you tapped into within yourself to effect that change.
> 3. Which Mini Miens within you did you embody to access those resources?
> 4. Take some time to map how you can use these Mini Miens and resources to instigate positive change towards your future goals.

Summary

Our personalities have a myriad of aspects: our Mini Miens. These have a significant impact on how we live our lives:

- Some fear-based experiences can activate specific Mini Miens to help us cope with difficult situations, but if we become too attached to these, they may disempower us in the long term.

- The Mini Miens we embody most frequently have shaped the results we have achieved thus far, but we have the power to choose new, more helpful Mini Miens for our future.

- Be selective about which Mini Miens you allow airtime to in your self-talk; they need to be the right ones for the situation you are in.

EIGHT
Day Seven: Making A Habit Of It

A habit can be described as a practice, a pattern or a routine. Now that we have reached Day Seven, it is important to remind ourselves that change will not happen without practice and creating new habits. We all have good habits and bad habits, with a large impact or a limited impact on our lives. Strangely, when we think about habits we tend to focus on the bad ones that need changing rather than the good habits that we could create.

When we initially learn habits, they are generally run by the subconscious mind, thus becoming automatic responses. By revisiting the daily lessons and exercises in this book, you will start to embed the changes you make as habits.

Physical and emotional habits

Habits can be physical or emotional. In terms of physical habits, these would include the specific way you change gears or use your indicator when driving, and the exact way you brush your hair or open a door. All of these are functional habits that help you get through your day without having to consciously remind yourself how to do these things each time the need arises. Other physical habits include nail-biting, smoking and using rude gestures. Although not massively destructive, most people would consider these bad habits.

The second type of habit is emotional habit. The emotional habits of, for example, feeling angry, anxious, fearful or sad on a regular basis have a direct impact on your behaviour. Anger can lead to physical violence; sadness can lead to lethargy; anxiety can lead to frustration and even physical violence or self-harm.

Emotional habits become engrained through an event or the memory of an event when a person responds to something that is happening with heightened emotion. This creates a neural pathway that supports that emotional response, which is repeated again and again until it gets strongly embedded. It is then easy to trigger, and the emotional habit kicks into action before the person is even aware of it.

When we change our emotional habits we can change our behaviour, our life and the lives of others around us, in a heartbeat. It can have a profound impact on our overall wellbeing and happiness. The next exercise will guide you through a process of identifying and starting to change an emotional habit that is not serving you well. By increasing self-awareness and implementing positive strategies, you can shift your emotional patterns and cultivate healthier responses.

> **EXERCISE: Emotional habits**
>
> Take a moment to reflect on an emotional habit that you would like to change. It could be something like impulsiveness, self-criticism, excessive worry or outbursts of anger. Write down the emotional habit you want to address, and then take the following steps:
>
> 1. **Identify the triggers:** think about the situations that commonly lead to the expression of the identified emotional habit. Reflect on the patterns and circumstances that bring it to the surface. Write down at least three specific triggers that are associated with it.
>
> 2. **Consider the consequences:** how does this emotional habit affect your wellbeing, relationships and overall quality of life? Reflect on the negative impacts it has on various aspects of your life. Write down the consequences you wish to avoid or change.
>
> 3. **Create new positive responses:** focus on transforming your emotional habit into a healthier response. Identify alternative ways to respond to the triggers, including identifying

which Mini Mien you could adopt when you anticipate being triggered.

4. **Practise and reinforce:** changing emotional habits takes effort and practice. Commit to identifying Mini Miens that support you and, using your hourly chime (from the 'Positive expectation' exercise in Chapter Two), associate into them hourly to begin with, so that you start to embed the new habit.

Starting with small steps and gradually building up your skills will help you achieve great results. Monitor your progress and celebrate every small victory along the way.

Feelings call the shots

If you are male, don't even think about skipping this section. We often believe that women are emotional and men are less so. That is not true. All of us are emotional, all of the time. In every moment of every day, we are all feeling something. This can be a heightened emotion or a feeling of being on an even keel, but we are still feeling something. Our feelings and emotions instigate all of our behaviours. Everything we do is at some level aimed at trying to feel better, as we discovered when learning about the Seven Behavioural Codes.

If you decide to go for a run, it is not necessarily because you want to feel only the physical benefits;

DAY SEVEN: MAKING A HABIT OF IT

you also want to feel the emotion that being fit brings you. It might be that you want to avoid feeling guilty (a fear of feeling guilt) or shame at not being fit, or, on the positive side, you might be driven by the emotions of joy, elation or freedom that come from feeling physically fit and healthy.

It's the same if you want to buy a car. You may think that you decide to do this because you need something to get you from A to B, and, yes, that is how the process begins. However, how will having a car and being able to easily get from A to B make you feel? Our feelings are the reason we are specific in our choices. The decision you make about the specifications of the car you want to buy will directly correlate to how you want that car to make you feel. It might be a need for economy, flashiness or seven seats, but whatever it is, you want those specifications because you want to feel something. An economical model may make you feel thrifty; something flashy might make you feel that you look good; and seven seats may enable you to feel relaxed in the knowledge that you can carry more passengers. It is the feeling that drives the decision.

The more you become aware of what is behind your behaviour (and indeed the feelings you are trying to fulfil by carrying out certain behaviours), the quicker and easier it will be to modify disempowering behaviours and ramp up the ones that serve you on every level. For now, just become aware of your behaviours and ask yourself if they are supporting you in creating the life you deserve.

Comfort zone

One feeling that rarely serves us is fear of stepping out of our comfort zone. This is the psychological and emotional space where we feel at ease, secure and familiar. It is a place where we experience minimal stress because we are safe within the boundaries of what we know and are comfortable with. We have a comfort zone in many aspects of life, including our routines, habits, relationships and environments. It acts as a protective barrier, guarding us from the potential challenges, risks or uncertainties that exist outside its boundaries. While it does provide a sense of stability and reassurance, it can also be a place where we experience frustration, boredom and limited personal growth, preventing us from exploring new opportunities. Stepping outside our comfort zone is often necessary to embrace change, learn new skills and achieve personal development and success.

For many clients I've seen over the years, an unconscious fear of stepping out of their comfort zone was related to a more specific fear of the vastness of the unknown that existed outside it. To support clients with this, I devised a simple technique that showed exceptional results. If you are stuck in your comfort zone, it can help you too.

DAY SEVEN: MAKING A HABIT OF IT

EXERCISE: Enlarge your comfort zone

To complete this exercise, you must first identify an area of your life in which you are stuck in a comfort zone. Get a piece of paper, a pencil and an eraser, and then:

1. Write a list of what is uncomfortable about staying stuck in this comfort zone.
2. Write a list of your fears of stepping out of it.
3. Draw a small square on a piece of paper and draw a stick person (you) inside the square.
4. Notice that the fear of the unknown and the uncertainties that exist in the vastness of the abyss outside that small square are what is holding you back.
5. Draw a second, bigger square around the one that has you in it.
6. Now erase 'you' from the inner square and draw a new you in the outer box.
7. Note that the bigger square that you are now in is outside your current comfort zone.
8. Now list some actions, behaviours and goals for this new square that will stretch you beyond your current comfort zone to create excitement, but not paralyse you with fear.

This larger square should challenge you and be a little uncomfortable, but you will experience immediate relief from not feeling you need to step into the abyss of the unknown on the rest of the page with no boundaries.

Of course, when you get comfortable within this new square you will again be stuck in a comfort zone. At this point, draw a new square around the first two and repeat the exercise.

Protection in difficult relationships

We all have people and relationships in our lives that we find difficult to manage. When we are in the company of these people, it can often be draining and extremely stressful. A way of describing what happens in these situations is that we become consumed by their stress, fear, anger or manipulation of us, or we react to their behaviour in a way that causes us stress. When this happens, we can leave the situation feeling depleted, low, frustrated, not in control, anxious or angry.

To protect yourself and stay emotionally regulated, there are ways to stay in the interaction while still retaining your power. The next exercise will help you in these situations. When you've learned it, don't limit its use just to these situations, but identify other areas where it can support you.

You can prime your RAS (which I introduced you to on Day One) to be aware of situations and people where this technique can be used. Doing so will help you to become subconsciously aware that you don't want to fall into the old default programme of reacting or becoming stressed in the situation. To achieve this, you will need to move from being unconsciously incompetent (your current state, before learning the exercise), to becoming unconsciously competent. This will require practice and patience.

> **EXERCISE: The Pink Bow**
>
> Take a moment to identify someone with whom you get stressed and deregulated, repeating a pattern that has played out time and again. It could be a difficult boss, a controlling work colleague, a stressed relative, a thoughtless friend or an unkind acquaintance. Just this initial step of becoming aware will prime your RAS to be alert in the future when a difficult situation arises so that you can subconsciously choose to react or respond differently. Then, next time you encounter the person and situation you have identified:
>
> - As the person in the situation starts to display the behaviour that stresses and deregulates you, take a conscious breath.
> - See their stress, anger, criticism, overwhelm and fear coming at you like a wave of energy.
> - In your mind's eye, notice how you can take a virtual step back.
> - Now imagine you are holding out your hands in front of you and let all of that person's stress, anger, criticism, overwhelm and fear sit on your hands – but do not let it wash over or consume you.
> - Let them finish what they are saying or doing while you still hold the stress in your hands.

- When they have finished, imagine yourself wrapping up all of that stress, anger, criticism, overwhelm and fear in beautiful wrapping paper, putting a big pink bow on it, and then imagine handing it back to that person.

To help you get comfortable with this exercise, practise before the situation arises. Do this by imagining the scenario and how you reacted in the past, and notice how stressed you felt and rate the feeling on a scale of one to ten for how intense it was. Then, reimagine the same scenario, applying the Pink Bow technique and notice how your stress response is greatly reduced. It doesn't matter that this is an imaginary scenario, your subconscious does not distinguish between imagining something and actually experiencing it. As a result, we respond emotionally and react to what we imagine. This is great because it means this technique can keep you emotionally regulated in challenging situations.

Golden Rule 6: People can only meet you where they are

Life will be easier for you if you are open to the idea that people are not inherently bad, but that *they can only meet you, understand you and behave from the level of consciousness or awareness that they are at.*

For some people, their level of awareness in life is, 'Bad things happen to me all the time', 'I have no choices',

'You are making me feel bad', 'It is your fault that I am this way.' This is living on the 'cause' side of an equation rather than the 'effect' side. Living from 'cause' awareness means the person can't take responsibility for their change, growth or possibilities because they don't know how – or even that they can. When someone is living at this level of awareness and can't see it, it is difficult for them to understand your perspective if you are living from the other side of the equation, ie, the effect side. They are not even aware that it exists, that this is possible.

On the 'effect' side, we are aware that we are responsible for how we feel and that change is possible. When we take responsibility for that change, we can transform our reality. We know that it takes effort, but we are willing to make that effort because we are committed to living our best life as well as supporting others to do the same. From this place, we can have compassion and understanding for someone who is on the 'cause' side of the equation.

The energy of words

One concept that will greatly enhance your capacity to choose the right side of the equation to live on, is the energy of words.

Language holds immense power. The words we use not only shape our perception of reality but also influence the way we experience life. By choosing our words wisely, we can cultivate a more positive and empowering inner dialogue. This, in turn, enhances our emotional wellbeing and boosts our overall mood.

The language we employ, whether in our internal or outward dialogue, has an impact on our energy and emotions. Becoming aware of this allows us to use it to our advantage. When we use expressions like, 'I should do' or 'I have to', we create a sense of obligation and external pressure. These imply that we are doing something out of necessity or because someone else expects it from us. This mindset can make us feel trapped, resentful, even rebellious – as if our freedom of choice is being taken away.

The truth is that we always have a choice, even in situations where it may not seem obvious. By becoming aware of our language and consciously choosing to use different words, we can shift our perspective and reclaim our power. Instead of using phrases that drain our energy, like 'I have to', we can reframe our thoughts and say, 'I choose to.'

This acknowledges our autonomy and personal agency. It reflects our ability to make decisions based on our values, desires and priorities. By recognising that we have a choice, we take ownership of our actions and embrace a proactive mindset.

This simple shift in language can have a profound effect on our emotional state and level of regulation.

When we say, 'I choose to', the energy changes. We no longer feel forced or obligated; instead, we feel a sense of freedom and empowerment.

The way we speak to ourselves matters. By consciously choosing empowering words, we can lift our spirits, boost our motivation and create a more positive and fulfilling life experience.

> **EXERCISE: Changing the energy with words**
>
> Take a few moments to find a quiet and comfortable space where you can reflect. Then, follow these steps:
>
> 1. Think of a task or responsibility that you feel obligated to do or have been putting off. Write down a brief description of this task, using phrases like 'I should do', 'I have to' and 'I must do', and how this makes you feel.
>
> 2. Take a deep breath and shift your perspective. Reframe your thoughts and rewrite your description of the task using the phrase 'I choose to'. Focus on the reasons why you want to do this task and how it aligns with your values, goals or wellbeing. Notice the changes in your emotions or energy compared to your previous feelings.
>
> 3. Compare the two descriptions. Take a moment to reflect on the differences in how you feel when using phrases of obligation versus those of choice. Notice any shifts in your mindset

> or emotional response. Write down all the insights and realisations that come to you.
>
> 4. Now consider how you can integrate the power of choice into your daily life. Think about other situations or responsibilities in relation to which you can consciously reframe your language from obligation to choice. Write down a few examples and imagine the positive effect this shift could have on your overall wellbeing and attitude.
>
> Remember, the words you use have the power to shape your experiences. Choose them wisely and consciously to create a more positive and fulfilling journey.

Summary

We may be all too aware of habits such as nail-biting or smoking, but we also need to consider how emotional habits may be affecting our lives:

- We all develop emotional habits as we go through life. Some are not supportive of our overall wellbeing and happiness, and changing them can have a profound impact.

- Emotional states drive our behaviour. Becoming aware of our emotions and miens can help us align our behaviour to bring joy, happiness and growth.

- Staying in our comfort zone limits personal growth and prevents us from exploring new opportunities. Step out of your comfort zone incrementally, gradually expanding it to embrace new actions, behaviours and goals rather than attempting radical action that might be overwhelming.

- Interacting with certain individuals can be draining and stressful, but it's important to stay emotionally regulated. The Pink Bow exercise can be used to return unwanted stress, overwhelm, anger and fear to their source.

- You can only meet others at the level of consciousness they possess. Understanding this helps foster compassion and understanding when dealing with others who may have a different level of awareness.

- The power of language shapes our experiences. By consciously choosing our words, we can shift our mindset from a feeling of obligation to one of agency.

NINE
Onwards And Upwards

Now that you are aware of how you work on the inside and the steps you can take to self-regulate, it is time to look at some concepts that will support your positive results as you revisit and repeat the seven days over the coming weeks.

Embracing change

When you take on board all the techniques and practices you have learned in this book, you will be ready to move forward to a brighter future. Living your life in this new way will make achieving dreams and goals much easier and more enjoyable. Not only that, but you will notice that you start to feel different, too. More peaceful, in mind and heart.

I surveyed a cross-section of clients who have embraced and applied the principles I outline in this book. They all said that learning how to create peace of mind and peace of heart dramatically improved every aspect of their life and accelerated their journey towards achieving their desired outcomes. Peace of mind and peace of heart are the most important and beneficial states we can embody; this is the most precious gift you can give yourself.

As a result of applying the principles of the Seven-Day Positivity Project, you should expect to feel more tolerant, motivated, content, joyful, fun and relaxed. You should also expect to feel less stressed, anxious, fearful, overwhelmed and flat. You may wish to use this new state as a platform to achieve new goals and dreams. In the sections below, I give you some guidelines on how you can do this.

Your 'why'

Regardless of where you are right now or where you want to get to, if you don't know *why* you want to achieve something, or if your why is not big enough, the chances of making your desires a reality are slim.

I work with many clients who are stuck, and they often try to convince me that their why is to be a role model to their children. Another much-used why is to be financially free and feel secure. In both cases, the clients are usually not anywhere near achieving their goals. On closer inspection, although they have a 'why', their desire is not strong enough. A person's subconscious desire, or need, to stay safe or comfortable, is usually what stops them from strengthening their why (first behavioural code).

Your desire to achieve something (your why) needs to be *much bigger than your fear of stepping out and taking the action*. This is incredibly important. Only when this balance is tipped will you be propelled to take disciplined action and get results.

I have experienced for myself the importance of a compelling 'why'.

I started smoking at the ripe old age of eleven. I continued through my teenage years, and when I started my nursing career my habit worsened. I used cigarettes as a stress reliever and also as a means of enjoyment while socialising. I smoked while having a coffee, meeting friends, between courses at meals, as soon as I got up in the morning and last thing at night. I remember once saying to a friend that I couldn't imagine life without cigarettes.

I tried giving up on several occasions and, although I truly wanted to, my *why*, the reason I wanted to give them up, was not big enough. In other words, the pain of smoking was not enough to outweigh the pain (fear) of giving up. To put it another way, the pleasure

I got from cigarettes was greater than the pleasure I would have gotten from the relief of giving them up.

If I had used sheer willpower to force myself, I could have stopped smoking. However, I would have been miserable because I would have felt deprived and would have been constantly fighting my desire to smoke. Instead, I had to ramp up the guilt I felt about smoking until it was unbearably uncomfortable and much stronger than my desire to smoke. I did this by embodying the aspect of my personality that felt guilty about smoking, my Health Freak Mini Mien, and using her self-talk to convince me. The more I did this, the louder she got and the stronger the guilt I felt became until it far outweighed the desire of my Comforter Mini Mien, who for years had used cigarettes to create a false sense of comfort.

I also tuned into the specific behavioural codes that my Comforter was trying to fulfil and began to understand where her need to smoke came from: the certainty that a cigarette would relax me (first code), the feeling of variety or selection when I smoked (second code) and, last but not least, the belief that cigarettes would provide comfort or self-love (fourth code). Once my feeling of guilt was greater than the need to fulfil these three codes my new 'why' not to smoke was far greater than my old 'why' to smoke.

I still remember the last cigarette I had, sitting by the Thames in London in 1993. As I put it out, I made a final decision – and I have never once smoked or even craved a cigarette since.

Your vision

To reap the benefits of following the principles in this book, it is important to have a plan, a goal and a North Star. I am not saying that you need to have a massive goal to strive towards. You're just looking for a road map, a direction in which you would like to take your life. Of course, if you do have a goal, big or small, now would be a good time to give it some attention so you can build in shape and detail.

Knowing your North Star

You must know what you want before you make any changes. The number of clients who proceed to tell me all that they *don't* want when I ask them what they want never ceases to amaze me. Remember when we were talking about your subconscious mind (Chapter Two) and how good it is at taking instruction? If you don't know what you want, your subconscious mind won't know how to get it for you.

I often liken this to taking a journey in a taxi. If the taxi driver doesn't know exactly where you want to go, they could end up taking you anywhere. Although this might work out fine, it would be better to plan before leaving so that there's no disappointment on arrival.

Even if the taxi driver knows the destination, the journey will not necessarily stay on course for the entire trip – there may be diversions or congestion. It is the same for you and your goals. It is OK to divert a little, as long as you have a map and compass so you can pull yourself back on track if you stray too far from the original path.

Decide to decide

Your next step is to decide, as it is the first step towards any result. We often underestimate the power of making an 'absolute' decision in one defining moment. Imagine drawing a line in the sand and deciding that today is the day things change. What would that do for your future?

Take some time to think about what you would like to change before you revisit the seven days. What would you like to be different or improved in your life? What areas would you like to change? What about your relationships, finances, health, social life, career or business?

Once you are clear on the area, next identify what specifically you wish to work on. Make a list of these things. Now it's time to formally decide to change – to create a moment where you make that decision purposefully. This provides your logical mind with a starting point so that it can work towards creating a middle and an end. Your logical mind performs best with order, so give it what it needs to get it working efficiently.

Who does this serve?

To ensure that your goal or vision comes to fruition, you need to check its ecology. The ecology is the effect that achieving this goal or vision might have on you, your family, your friends, your wider community and your environment.

Ask yourself: 'If I achieve this goal, will it be good for me, my family, my community and the broader circles of my world?' If the answer is yes, then it is ecologically sound. If the answer is no, review your options.

Getting your ducks in a row

Once you're clear on your vision and know that it is aligned with your goals and that your goals serve you, it's time to ensure you have all your 'ducks in a row' – your tools and resources lined up and ready to go.

The Seven Behavioural Codes

Ensure your goal is aligned with your positive outcome by taking some time to check it against your Seven Behavioural Codes. For each code, ask yourself: 'Will achieving this goal fulfil my code for...?' If you get a 'yes' on all seven codes, you are truly aligned with this goal. You will likely find it easy to achieve, and, as a bonus, it will bring you true happiness.

The Golden Rules

To support the dynamics of having other people involved in your goal, keep the six Golden Rules in this book at the forefront of your mind. Remember, other people's representations of the world will be different to yours. They may have the same vision or end goal but their interpretation of how to get there will most likely differ. By embracing the Golden Rules, you will be able to manage any discrepancies with limited stress and push forward with your plans. To recap:

- **Golden Rule 1:** Change your perception of reality.

- **Golden Rule 2:** Everyone has their own unique model of the world.

- **Golden Rule 3:** There is a positive intention behind all behaviour.

- **Golden Rule 4:** Practise non-judgement of others.

- **Golden Rule 5:** You have all the resources you need.

- **Golden Rule 6:** People can only meet you where they are at.

Mini Miens

Identify the Mini Miens (Day Six) with strengths that will best serve the execution of your goal. I generally use one or two miens for a specific goal; using more than two can get a bit loose and confusing.

When you are clear on these miens, condition yourself to embody them regularly. Initially, when I work on a goal, I set the chime app on my phone on an hourly basis to remind me to embody the mien that will support me. After a few days, I become more conditioned to the mien so I reduce the frequency of the chime to every three hours or so, and I continue to reduce it as the conditioning strengthens.

Get to the detail

In the 'Decide to decide' section earlier in this chapter, you made a list of the areas you want to change in your life. Now you need to get a little more specific in relating that to your goal. Decide what exactly you would like to be, do, or have in those areas, and most importantly, what you would like to *feel* when you are being, doing and having those things. If what you want to feel is not aligned with your goal, then your goal will never make you happy. Whether it's a business goal, relationship goal, health goal or financial goal, take time to focus on what you would like to *feel* in relation to this goal.

See it

Next, it is important to create a picture of what you want to change in your mind. Imagine you are standing in your bedroom. From where you are standing, is the bed in front of you or behind you, to the right or left? What colour are the walls? Paint a picture in your mind. Now imagine a big present wrapped up in beautiful paper, sitting on your bed.

It doesn't matter if the picture is not high definition, or even fully in focus. If you can see any of this in your mind's eye, then you can visualise. When your mind can picture your goal, it is easier to create a road or path to get to it. Practise seeing your goal, even if it seems a distance away from you.

Feel it

The next and even more critical piece is to feel your goal. If you struggle with visualising, the good news is that the feeling part is more important, and we generally find it easier.

To start feeling, imagine you have achieved your goal. Put yourself into the picture of having achieved the goal. Step into yourself in that picture and let it embody you. When you are ready, look out through your own eyes at that picture and see what you would see, hear what you would hear and start to feel what it would be like to have achieved that goal: the feelings inside your tummy, your heart, your head and in every cell of your being. Take your time and enjoy the feelings. The more you allow yourself to feel and to let those feelings intensify, the better able your subconscious mind will be to support you in achieving your goal.

Craft it

Vision boards have become popular in recent years, and I do think they are helpful. Let me briefly explain what a vision board is and then I will give you some helpful pointers for getting the best out of one.

A vision board is a mounting board, notice board, scrap book or any physical or online medium that allows you to post visual representations of the things you want to achieve or attract into your life. You can write or draw on the board or you can add cut-outs of images or text from magazines or the internet or your own photographs, or indeed you can create a digital board on your computer. These visual reminders of what you would like to have in your life keep both your conscious and subconscious minds alert to the behaviours that you need to execute to reach your goals.

I prefer words to images. I find it difficult to compute my visions from a generic picture of someone else's. It's important to find your own 'groove' and establish what is meaningful to you. That said, there is no point in just having a vision board. You have to feel what it will be like to have achieved what is on it so that your mind and body know what to move towards. Employ all of your senses for best results – use the technique from the 'Feel it' section above, starting by focusing in on any images on your vision board and imagining yourself stepping into them, making sure that you embody yourself in the image before looking out through your own eyes. Then focus in on any words on your vision board, and, similarly, see what you would see, hear what you would hear and feel what you would feel in relation to those words as you imagine that you have realised your goal.

Locking in your goal

When I am working towards a goal, I typically practise enjoying the feeling for a few minutes and then stepping out of the picture. Then, in my mind's eye, I put the goal in front of me at the specific point in my future by which I would like to have achieved it. That could be three months, six months or even a year.

Setting up your goal in this way will give you a frame of reference if procrastination sets in. I have already covered some ideas on how to overcome procrastination in Chapter Four; go back and review them if needed and then set up the feeling of this goal in the best way you possibly can.

Timeframe

It's important to have a timeframe for what you want to achieve. This will satisfy your mind. Knowing how long you intend the process to last will help you both consciously and subconsciously plan time blocks within the allocated period. I always start at the end and work back.

For example, let's say I decide I want to achieve a business goal within six months. I then ask myself what I need to have done by month five, month four, month three and so on. This helps me to map out the actions I need to take to achieve the goal within the desired timeframe. All the while, I'm also living according to the principles of the Seven-Day Positivity Project, so I'm fully aligned and, therefore, in the best possible position to achieve my goals.

If I had stayed the way I was twenty years ago, wrapped up in my insecurities, fears and worries, it would have been virtually impossible for me to create a good life. I am not saying I wouldn't have had some happiness, good health, a successful business and great people in my life, but I know deep down that I wouldn't have achieved what I have now.

Get your action steps down on paper and then transfer them into your calendar so that you are clear on what needs to be done and when.

Action in action

We're often advised to take massive action to get massive results. In itself, this advice is not necessarily wrong, but I think it is questionable for many reasons. I'm going to share some important insights about the types and qualities of action that I teach my clients. These will enable you to amplify your results by working smarter rather than harder.

1. Inspired action

There is little point in taking action and moving towards the future you have marked out for yourself if that future doesn't inspire you. This goes hand in hand with the concept of making your 'why' bigger than the fear of not achieving your vision. Inspiration moves mountains when it is aligned with our beliefs, values and Seven Behavioural Codes. Check in with yourself to see if you are genuinely inspired to take the action required.

2. Imperfect action

It is easy to be held back as we wait for the perfect time and the perfect conditions. We sometimes feel we need to study more so that we have perfect knowledge before moving forward. We wait for the perfect website, the perfect home, the perfect look, the perfect weight – the list goes on. Well, here's the deal: there is no such thing as perfect.

Many clients who were initially petrified of the concept of taking action in less-than-perfect circumstances decided to embrace imperfection, and they have since thanked me for encouraging them to do so. They may not have got the best results – but at least they got results. These results inspired them to take further action so that they got more results, and the quality of those results consistently improved. Those who were waiting for things to be perfect are still waiting, and nothing has changed.

Finally, I want to stress that although you may need to take action in less-than-ideal circumstances, you can still do so in a purposeful and committed way. Embracing imperfect, undeterred action need not mean compromising on your standards.

3. Complete action

So many people fly around like busy fools, taking massive action but not bringing projects to completion. Focusing on and finishing one thing at a time is one of the fastest ways to get results – though only if you are combining this execution with the other components of action-taking described here. Look at your goals and get clear on the next two to three actions you need to take to support you in getting the best results. Then, commit to completing them before taking any other actions.

4. Sensible action

Last but not least, make sure the action you are taking is going to contribute directly to realising your vision or goal. Check that all the steps within your action are sensible, targeted and will take you closer to achieving your desired outcome. Avoid adding in any unnecessary extra steps, and delegate or automate tasks where possible.

Summary

Embarking on the Seven-Day Positivity Project is the beginning of an exciting process of change and growth. Keep the following points in mind as you progress to enhance your enjoyment and your results:

- You must be open to embracing change if you want to move towards a brighter future.
- Having a strong 'why' is essential to increase motivation for achieving your goals.
- Setting a clear vision and knowing exactly what you want enables your subconscious to support you in getting there.
- Creating a formal moment where you make a conscious and purposeful decision to change is important for achieving positive results.

- To ensure you're aligned with your goals, check their ecology by considering whether they align with your Seven Behavioural Codes, bearing in mind the six Golden Rules and your Mini Miens.

- Visualising and feeling the achievement of your goals, setting a timeframe for them, and taking inspired, imperfect, complete and sensible action will support the execution of your goals and maximise your results.

Conclusion

The end is just the beginning. You now have the information, techniques, processes and concepts to transform your life in a powerful and meaningful way.

I encourage you to repeat the seven days for several weeks at least – each time you do, your learning and insights will go deeper.

It has been a pleasure and privilege to share the knowledge I have gained and the client stories I have witnessed over the years to help support your positive future. One of my favourite concepts in life is: 'None of us is ahead or behind, better or worse. We are all simply doing our best.' Keep this in mind as you progress.

Work with me

I understand that some people benefit enormously from reading a book and others like or need to avail themselves of extra help. I prefer to adopt a variety of methods when I am learning a new skill or process. If this is the same for you, there are many ways you can engage with me further, to deepen your learnings and speed up your transformation.

I offer many online programmes. I also host live events and run a certification programme to qualify students in QTT. If you would like to avail yourself of some of the free lifechanging content I share, visit my website www.moirageary.com and click the 'Start Here' button.

With so many opportunities to stay connected, I hope that we will meet again soon.

My final message

People who are attracted to personal development, self-help or spiritual growth books are generally hoping to change for the better in some way. On the journey, we often subconsciously put ourselves under pressure to feel better and to get the results we are seeking. I hope every word in this book will enable you to achieve those positive results in some way – but please be careful not to try and change things that don't need to change.

You don't have to change a disempowering belief unless you want to. You can wallow in your Victim Mini Mien for as long as you're happy to. If you are holding onto sadness, hurt, guilt or any other negative emotion, you don't have to change that either. You decide what needs to change, when it needs to change and how you want to change it. No pressure.

With much love,

Moira

Notes

1. V Taschereau-Dumouchel, A Cortese, T Chiba, *et al.*, 'Towards an unconscious neural reinforcement intervention for common fears', *Proceedings of the National Academy of Sciences of the United States of America*, 115/13 (2018), 3470–3475, https://doi.org/10.1073/pnas.1721572115, accessed 10 April 2024
2. L Adams, 'Learning a new skill is easier said than done' (Gordon Training International, 2015), www.gordontraining.com/free-workplace-articles/learning-a-new-skill-is-easier-said-than-done, accessed 10 April 2024
3. WB Davidson and PR Cotter, 'The relationship between sense of community and subjective well-being: A first look', *Journal of Community*

Psychology, 19/3 (1991), 246–253, https://doi.org/10.1002/1520-6629(199107)19:3<246::AID-JCOP2290190308>3.0.CO;2-L, accessed 10 April 2024

4 ML Kern, SS Della Porta and HS Friedman, 'Lifelong pathways to longevity: Personality, relationships, flourishing, and health', *Journal of Personality,* 82/6 (2013), 472–484, https://doi.org/10.1111/jopy.12062, accessed 10 April 2024

5 YC Yang, C Boen, K Gerken, *et al.,* 'Social relationships and physiological determinants of longevity across the human life span', *Proceedings of the National Academy of Sciences of the United States of America,* 113/3 (2016), 578–583, https://doi.org/10.1073/pnas.1511085112, accessed 10 April 2024

6 CE Ackerman, 'What is positive psychology and why is it important?' (Positive Psychology, 20 April 2018), https://positivepsychology.com/what-is-positive-psychology-definition, accessed 21 March 2024

7 J Nash, 'The 5 founding fathers and a history of positive psychology' (Positive Psychology, 12 February 2015), https://positivepsychology.com/founding-fathers, accessed 21 March 2024

8 Pursuit of Happiness.org, 'Martin Seligman and Positive Psychology: Theory and practice' (Pursuit of Happiness, 2024), www.pursuit-of-happiness.org/history-of-happiness/martin-seligman-psychology, accessed 10 April 2024

Psychology, 19/3 (1991), 246–253, https://doi.org/10.1002/1520-6629(199107)19:3<246::AID-JCOP2290190308>3.0.CO;2-L, accessed 10 April 2024

4   ML Kern, SS Della Porta and HS Friedman, 'Lifelong pathways to longevity: Personality, relationships, flourishing, and health', *Journal of Personality*, 82/6 (2013), 472–484, https://doi.org/10.1111/jopy.12062, accessed 10 April 2024

5   YC Yang, C Boen, K Gerken, *et al.*, 'Social relationships and physiological determinants of longevity across the human life span', *Proceedings of the National Academy of Sciences of the United States of America*, 113/3 (2016), 578–583, https://doi.org/10.1073/pnas.1511085112, accessed 10 April 2024

6   CE Ackerman, 'What is positive psychology and why is it important?' (Positive Psychology, 20 April 2018), https://positivepsychology.com/what-is-positive-psychology-definition, accessed 21 March 2024

7   J Nash, 'The 5 founding fathers and a history of positive psychology' (Positive Psychology, 12 February 2015), https://positivepsychology.com/founding-fathers, accessed 21 March 2024

8   Pursuit of Happiness.org, 'Martin Seligman and Positive Psychology: Theory and practice' (Pursuit of Happiness, 2024), www.pursuit-of-happiness.org/history-of-happiness/martin-seligman-psychology, accessed 10 April 2024

Notes

1 V Taschereau-Dumouchel, A Cortese, T Chiba, *et al.*, 'Towards an unconscious neural reinforcement intervention for common fears', *Proceedings of the National Academy of Sciences of the United States of America*, 115/13 (2018), 3470–3475, https://doi.org/10.1073/pnas.1721572115, accessed 10 April 2024

2 L Adams, 'Learning a new skill is easier said than done' (Gordon Training International, 2015), www.gordontraining.com/free-workplace-articles/learning-a-new-skill-is-easier-said-than-done, accessed 10 April 2024

3 WB Davidson and PR Cotter, 'The relationship between sense of community and subjective well-being: A first look', *Journal of Community*

9 K Douglas, 'The subconscious mind: Your unsung hero', *New Scientist* (28 November 2007), www.newscientist.com/article/mg19626321-400-the-subconscious-mind-your-unsung-hero, accessed 21 March 2024

10 S van Gaal and VAF Lamme, 'Unconscious high-level information processing: Implication for neurobiological theories of consciousness', *Neuroscientist*, 18/3 (2011), 287–301, https://pubmed.ncbi.nlm.nih.gov/21628675/

11 D Centonze, A Siracusano, P Calabresi, *et al.*, 'Removing pathogenic memories', *Molecular Neurobiology*, 32 (2005), 123–132, https://doi.org/10.1385/MN:32:2:123, accessed 10 April 2024

12 HT Blair, GE Schafe, EP Bauer, *et al.*, 'Synaptic plasticity in the lateral amygdala: A cellular hypothesis of fear conditioning', *Learning Memory*, 8 (2001), 229–242, www.learnmem.org/cgi/doi/10.1101/lm.30901, accessed 10 April 2024

13 A Vaish, T Grossmann and A Woodward, 'Not all emotions are created equal: The negativity bias in social-emotional development', *Psychological Bulletin*, 134/3 (2008), 383–403, https://doi.org/10.1037/0033-2909.134.3.383, accessed 10 April 2024

14 A Vaish, T Grossmann and A Woodward, 'Not all emotions are created equal: The negativity bias in social-emotional development', *Psychological Bulletin*, 134/3 (2008), 383–403, https://doi.org/10.1037/0033-2909.134.3.383

15 R Hanson, *Hardwiring Happiness* (Harmony, 2013), https://rickhanson.com/writings/books/hardwiring-happiness

16 A Takayama and H Sekiya, 'Effects of various sitting and standing postures on arousal and valence', *PLoS One*, 18/6 (2023), e0286720, https://doi.org/10.1371/journal.pone.0286720

17 N McDermott, 'The mental health benefits of gratitude' (Forbes, 10 November 2023), www.forbes.com/health/mind/mental-health-benefits-of-gratitude, accessed 21 March 2024

18 E Garcia-Rill, 'Chapter 1: Waking and the reticular activating system in health and disease', in Edgar Garcia-Rill, ed, *Governing Principles of Brain Activity* (Academic Press, 2015), www.sciencedirect.com/book/9780128013854/waking-and-the-reticular-activating-system-in-health-and-disease

19 C Hounslow, 'Reticular activating system: Intention in attention' (Contemporary Psychology, 2024), www.contemporarypsychology.com.au/reticular-activating-system-intention-in-attention, accessed 10 April 2024

20 The Mayo Clinic, 'Chronic stress puts your health at risk' (Mayo Clinic, 1 August 2023), www.mayoclinic.org/healthy-lifestyle/stress-management/in-depth/stress/art-20046037, accessed 21 March 2024

21 KT Larkin, LA Brown and AG Tiani, 'Chapter 5: Autonomic and neuroendocrine response to stress', in Paul D Chantler and Kevin T Larkin,

eds, *Cardiovascular Implications of Stress and Depression* (Academic Press, 2020) pp87–110, https://doi.org/10.1016/B978-0-12-815015-3.00005-2

22 O Guy-Evans, 'Amygdala hijack: How it works, signs, and how to cope' (Simply Psychology, 18 September 2023), www.simplypsychology.org/amygdala-hijack.html, accessed 21 March 2024

23 K Cherry, 'Maslow's hierarchy of needs' (Very Well Mind, 14 August 2022), www.verywellmind.com/what-is-maslows-hierarchy-of-needs-4136760, accessed 21 March 2024

24 HT Blair, GE Schafe, EP Bauer, *et al.*, 'Synaptic plasticity in the lateral amygdala: A cellular hypothesis of fear conditioning', *Learning and Memory*, 8/5 (2001), 229–242, doi.org/10.1101/lm.30901, accessed 10 April 2024

25 Britannica Dictionary (2024), www.britannica.com/science/memory-psychology

26 A Okros, *Harnessing the Potential of Digital Post-Millennials in the Future Workplace* (Springer, 2020), pp37–38

27 OED: Oxford English Dictionary (2024), www.oed.com/search/advanced/Meanings?textTerm Text0=judgemental

28 OED: Oxford English Dictionary (2024), www.oed.com/dictionary/mien_n1

29 S McVey, '6 steps to parts integration' (International NLP Association, 19 February 2021), https://internationalnlpassociation.org/pull-yourself-together-6-steps, accessed 21 March 2024

Acknowledgements

I would like to thank every single person I have had the privilege to connect with, virtually and in person since the day I landed on this earth. Each encounter, good or bad, has in some way been instrumental in helping me uncover and formalise the concepts in *The Seven-Day Positivity Project*.

Closer to home, big 'thank you' hugs to my four favourite men: my husband Jeff and my three boys, Joe, Dan and Conor. Patience, tolerance and love would go a long way in describing your input.

A special mention and massive gratitude to Verity Ridgman, my writing coach, and my many beta readers, especially Vig Gleeson and Mary O'Neill, for their incredible feedback as well as the love and support that helped transform my ideas and words into this beautiful project. I could not have put this together without them.

The Author

Moira Geary is an ordinary woman with a rare and proven ability to help people achieve extraordinary results. She is the 'been there, done that' girl, working with people to overcome what she has overcome herself. The fact that she has personally experienced and overcome adversity, she believes, is paramount to her ability to show others how to be happy and successful.

Mum to three young men and wife to Jeff, Moira has gained formal training and experience in many modalities. Her academic awards include a master's degree in psychotherapy, a professional diploma in positive health, general nursing and midwifery as well as many other holistic modalities. Moira is an expert in cognitive reimprinting and neurological repatterning and has worked with the world's leading mind experts as well as running her own highly successful personal development company. Moira is a regular contributor to the media and, over the last twenty years, has taught thousands of people globally how to manage stress and fear so that they can create the good life they deserve.

Get in touch with Moira at:

🌐 www.moirageary.com

📷 www.instagram.com/moirageary_

📘 www.facebook.com/Iammoirageary

💼 www.linkedin.com/in/moirageary

Join Moira's free supportive community: www.moirageary.com/community

If you would like to enquire about becoming a Quantum Thinking Transformation® Practitioner please send an email to support@moirageary.com

Milton Keynes UK
Ingram Content Group UK Ltd.
UKHW020642280824
447523UK00005B/298